D1452723

THE CHURCH AND THE CATHOLIC

THE SPIRIT OF THE LITURGY

THE CHURCH AND THE CATHOLIC

AND

THE SPIRIT OF THE LITURGY

BY

ROMANO GUARDINI

TRANSLATED BY

ADA LANE

NEW YORK

SHEED & WARD INC.

1953

NIHIL OBSTAT : INNOCENTIUS APAP, S.TH.M. ; O.P.
CENSOR DEPUTATUS

IMPRIMATUR : ✠ JOSEPH BUTT
VIC. GEN.

WESTMONASTERII, DIE 27A IULII 1935

CONTENTS

THE CHURCH AND THE CATHOLIC

THE SPIRIT OF THE LITURGY

THE CHURCH AND THE CATHOLIC

THE CHURCH AND THE CATHOLIC

I

THE AWAKENING OF THE CHURCH IN THE SOUL

A RELIGIOUS process of incalculable importance has begun—the Church is coming to life in the souls of men.

This must be correctly understood. The Church has, of course, been continuously alive in herself, and at all times of decisive importance for her members. They have accepted her teaching, obeyed her commands ; her invincible vitality has been their strong support and the ground of their trust. But, with the development of individualism since the end of the Middle Ages, the Church has been thought of as a means to true religious life—as it were a God-designed framework or vessel in which that life is contained—a viaduct of life but not as life itself.[1] It has, in other words, been thought of as a thing exterior from which men might receive life, not a thing into which men must be incorporated that they may live with its life.

[1] This and the remarks which follow are intended merely to describe how people felt and what consciousness was theirs. It is not concerned with the essence and significance of the Church herself.

Religious life tended increasingly away from the community and towards the individual sphere. The Church, therefore, came to be regarded as the boundary of this sphere, and perhaps even as its opponent. In any case the Church was felt as a power fettering personality and thereby restricting the religious life. And this external regulation appeared either beneficent, or inevitable, or oppressive, according to the disposition of the individual.

This is inevitably a one-sided presentation. Actually there were very many exceptions; transition and development made the picture far more complicated. Nor was this attitude to the Church without its greatness. To-day all the catchwords of the age are against it: but we should ask nevertheless what valuable contributions it has made to religious life as a whole. Perhaps it is the right moment to do so, just because we inwardly stand apart from it and can therefore look at it objectively.

What was the basis of this attitude? The answer has already been indicated—the subjectivism and individualism of the modern age.

Religion was considered as something which belonged to the subjective sphere—it was simply something within a man, a condition of his soul. We are not speaking of conscious scientific theories, but of the spiritual tendency of the age. Objective religion represented by the Church was for the individual primarily the regulation of this individual and subjective religion; a protection against its inadequacies. That which remained over and above— the objective religion in its disinterested sublimity, and the community as a value in itself often left the individual cold and aroused no response in his heart. Even the acceptance and the enthusiasm which the Church evoked were largely external and individualistic, and psychologically had a strong affinity with the earlier ' patriotism.' When we look more closely we see that often enough there was no genuine belief in the existence of objective religious realities. This subjectivism dominated religious life all through the second half of the nineteenth century and during the beginning of the twentieth. Man felt imprisoned within himself. That is why from Kant onwards, and particularly in the more recent idealism, the problem of knowledge became so urgent—indeed for many it constituted the whole of philosophy ! The man of this age considered the very existence of an *object* as doubtful. He was not directly and strongly conscious of the reality of things, at bottom indeed not even of his own. Such intellectual systems as consistent solipsism did not rest upon logical conclusions, but were tentative interpretations of this personal experience. It is impossible to explain on purely intellectual grounds such philosophies as the new idealism for which the subject is a mere logical entity. They arose from the attempt to replace the objective reality of things, which had become doubtful, by a logical reality. Thus originated the conception of the *a priori* as having objective validity logically, although its subjective validity was only empirical ; and the doctrine that experience is based upon the subject and not upon the thing, and similar forms of philosophic subjectivism. The primary experience of reality was lacking. Sometimes this fact would suddenly dawn upon a student of philosophy when a leading representative of the new idealism declared, in a University for example, that ' Being ' is a ' value ' ! It would be impossible to express more shortly or more bluntly how impossible this attitude was, and how it could only have originated in a profound spiritual impotence. Reality as experienced had no longer any solidity or force. It was a lifeless shadow. And in this philosophy did but translate into its formulas and its idiom what all felt in one way or another. In spite of the much vaunted 'realism,' in spite of natural science, technical achievement, and a realist politics, man could not see the real object, the finished article, nor even himself. He lived in an intermediate sphere between being and nothingness, among concepts and mechanisms, among formulas and systems, which sought to represent and control objects, but which were not even coherent. He lived in a world of abstract forms and symbols, which was not linked up with the reality to which the symbols referred. We are reminded of a wholesale manufacturer, who knows exactly what workmen, officials, buyers, and contractors he employs, and has particulars of the whole in his register, including descriptions of all his raw materials and goods, labelled in the most accurate methods of physico-chemical research—but who knows nothing of his employees as human beings, and has no innate feeling for fine material or good work.

This attitude was also making its influence felt in the religious sphere. Nothing which was not an immediate experience or a logical datum had power to convince, was accepted without further question. The individual was sure only of that which he personally experienced, perceived, and yearned for, and on the other hand of the concepts, ideas, and postulates of his own thought. Consequently the Church was of necessity experienced not as a self-justified religious reality, but as the limiting value of the subjective; not as a living body, but as a formal institution.[1]

Religious life was thus individualistic, disintegrated, and unsocial. The individual lived for himself. 'Myself and my Creator' was for many the exclusive formula. The community was not primary; it took the second place. It no longer was a natural reality which existed from the first by its own right. It had to be thought out, willed, and deliberately set up. One individual, it was believed, approached another, and went into partnership with him. But he was not from the outset bound up with a group of his fellows, the member of an organic community, sharing its common life. There was indeed no community, merely a mechanical organisation, and this in the religious sphere as in every other. How little in Divine worship were the faithful aware of themselves as a community! How inwardly disintegrated the community was! How little was the individual parishioner conscious of the parish, and in how individualistic a spirit was the very Sacrament of community—Communion—conceived!

This attitude was intensified by another factor—the rationalistic temper of the age. That alone was admitted which could be 'comprehended' and 'calculated.' The attempt was made to substitute for the properties of things, as given in indissoluble unity of the concrete object, mathematically defined groups of relations; to replace life by chemical formulas. Instead of the soul, people talked about psychic processes. The living unity of

[1] Naturally much in this individualism is necessary and true. These criticisms are directed solely against a false one-sidedness which impoverishes human life; against subjectivism, not against the subjective. This will be obvious from all that follows.

personality was viewed as a bundle of events and activities. The age was in direct contact only with that which could be demonstrated by experiment. That something lay behind what was perceptible to the senses had first of all to be made credible by a distinct process of reflection. Already the mysterious depths of individual personality, whatever moved and lived in the soul, was being questioned. And the supra-personal unity of the community was not seen at all. The community was regarded as a mere aggregate of individuals, as an organisation of ends and means. Its mysterious substance, its creative power, and the organic laws governing communal growth and development, remained inaccessible.

All this naturally exerted its influence upon men's conception of the Church. She appeared above all as a legal institution for religious purposes. There was no limit perception of the mystical element in her, everything in fact which lies behind her palpable aims and visible institutions, and is expressed by the concept of the kingdom of God, the mystical Body of Christ.

* * * * *

This entire attitude, however, is now undergoing a profound change. New forces are at work busy in those mysterious depths of human nature where the intellectual and spiritual movements which now shape the life of a human culture receive their origin and direction. We are conscious of reality as a primary fact. It is no longer something dubious from which it is advisable to retreat upon the logical validity which seems more solid and more secure. Reality is as solid, indeed more solid, because prior, richer and more comprehensive. Proofs are accumulating that people are willing to accept concrete reality as the one self-evident fact, and to base abstract truth upon it. We need not be astonished at this new Nominalism. The consciousness of reality has burst upon mankind with the force of a new and a personal experience. Our age is literally rediscovering that things exist, and moreover with an individuality incalculable, because creative and original. The concrete, in its boundless fulness, is being once more experienced, and the happiness of being able to venture oneself to it and enter into it. It is experienced as freedom and wealth—I am real, and so also is this thing which confronts one in its self-determined abundance ! And thought is a living relation between myself and it—perhaps, who knows, also between it and myself ? Action is a real communication with it. Life is a real self-development, a progress among things, a communion with realities, a mutual give and take. That extreme critical aloofness which was formerly considered the acme of rationality, is becoming more and more incomprehensible to us, a stupefying dream, which imprisoned man in an empty, dead world of concepts, cut off from the luxuriant life of the real world. Modern idealism—against which the assaults of logic were so long delivered in vain, because the foundation of the system was not proof, but a dogmatic foundation of the mental attitude of the entire age—no longer needs to be refuted. The bottom has fallen out of it. Its spell is broken, and we ask ourselves how it is that we endured it so long. A great awakening to reality is in progress.

And it is an awakening moreover to metaphysical reality. I do not believe that any man who is not tenaciously persisting, is not clinging to an attitude adopted long before, any man who is living in the age or even in advance of it, any longer seriously doubts the reality of the soul. Already there has been talk of a 'world of spiritual objects,' that is to say, the psychic is experienced as sufficiently real to necessitate our acceptance of an entire order of being beyond the sensible. The more difficult task for the scientist is now to make the transition from the former denial, which had become a scientific article of faith, to the inevitable admission of the self-evident fact that the soul exists. And the existence of God is equally self-evident. Spiritualism and anthropo-sophy—in themselves so unsatisfactory—prove how powerful the consciousness of metaphysical reality has already become. In the face of such movements we find ourselves obliged to defend the pure spirituality of God and of the soul, while upholding the reality in their own order of empirical objects. And the revival of a Platonic type of thought points in the same direction. Spiritual forms are again viewed as metaphysical forces, and no longer as merely involved in the logical structure of con-sciousness. And many other signs of the same tendency could be adduced.

Community is admitted just as directly. The attitude of withdrawal into the barred fortress of self no longer passes, as it did twenty years ago, for the only noble attitude. On the contrary, it is regarded as unjustifiable, barren and impotent. Just as powerful as the experience that things exist and the world exists, is the experience that human beings exist. Indeed, the latter is by far more powerful, because it affects us more closely. There are human beings like myself. Each one is akin to me, but each one is also a separate world of his own, of unique value. And from this realisation springs the passionate conviction that we all belong one to another; are all brothers. It is now taken as self-evident that the individual is a member of the community. The latter does not originate through one man attaching himself to another, or renouncing part of his independence. The community is just as primary a fact as individual existence. And the task of building up the community is just as primary and fundamental as that of perfecting personality.

And this consciousness of interdependence assures a most significant expression; it develops into the consciousness of nationality. 'The people' does not mean the masses, or the uncultured, or the 'primitives,' whose mental and spiritual life, and whose system of facts and values are as yet undeveloped. All these uses of the term derive from the ideas of liberalism, the *Aufklärung* and individualism. An entirely new note is now being sounded; something essential is being born. 'The people' is the primary association of those human beings who by race, country, and historical antecedents share the same life and destiny. The people is a human society which maintains an unbroken continuity with the roots of nature and life, and obeys their intrinsic laws. The people contains—not numerically or quantitatively, but in essential quality—the whole of mankind, in all its human variety of ages, sexes, temperament, mental and physical condition; to which we must add the sum total of its work and spheres of production as determined by class and vocation. The people is mankind in its radical comprehensiveness. And a man is of 'the people' if he embraces, so to speak, this whole within himself. His opposite number is the 'cultured' man. He is not the people, developed and intellectualised, but a malformation, a one-sided, debased and uprooted being. He is a product of humanism, and above all of the *Aufklärung*. He is a human type which has cut itself adrift from the ties which make man's physical and mental life organic. He has fallen away on the one hand into a world of abstraction, on the other into the purely physical sphere ; from union with nature into the purely scholastic and artificial ; from the community into isolation. His deepest longing should be to become once more one of the people ; not indeed by romantic attempts to conform with popular ideas and customs, but by a renewal of his inmost spirit by a progressive return to a simple and complete life. The Youth movement is an attempt in this direction.

And already a new reality is beginning to appear above the horizon. Here also the use of the word needs to be purified. It need not denote the rationalist conception of ' humanity,' but the living unity of the human race, of blood, destiny, responsibility, and labour ; that solidarity which is postulated by the dogma of original sin and vicarious redemption, mysteries which no rationalist can understand.

The individual self is conscious of enrichment not only by the experience of real things, but also by the community, which expands its self-consciousness into a consciousness of a communal self. By direct sympathy, what belongs to another becomes mine own, and what belongs to me becomes his.

The fully-formed community owes its existence to a combination between the awareness of objective reality and the communal consciousness. Law, justice, and the order of society are seen to be the forms by which the community exists and operates and maintains the ground of its stability. They are not limitations of life, but its presuppositions. They do not petrify it, but give it force and enable it to energise. They, of course, in turn, must be really genuinely alive. And profound changes will occur in the Social Structure, legal changes for example, as soon as the realisation becomes more general that a *matured* national community needs not an individualistic but a communal system of public law; not a system of abstract principles existing merely upon paper, but a system shaped by the vital growth of the community; that its constitution cannot be the product of abstract reasoning but must grow out of the real being and life of this people.[1]

In like manner the stream of life has burst its dams. Side by side with reason and on an equal footing with it stand the will, creative power and feeling. Being is given equal importance with doing, indeed greater. Development and growth rank with or above action; personality whose very reality was once called in question is accepted as the most obvious or familiar object of experience. Its incomprehensibility is a datum as primary as the logical comprehensibility of its abstract concept. And the problem to be solved is that of the relations between concept and intuition, theory and experience, being and action, form and life; the way in which one depends for

[1] At this point the real meaning of politics becomes clear. It is no technique of deceit, lying and violence. But it means the noble art which accepts all the concrete phenomena of life, races, classes, and without violating their distinctive characters finds room for all, but in such a fashion that their combined life and functions build up a powerful and richly endowed society. Here moral and educational problems intervene which, to the best of my knowledge, hardly anyone with the exception of F.W. Foerster has seriously tackled.

its existence upon the other, and unity is achieved by the conjunction of all these factors.

This life is also stirring in our consciousness of the community. We are as immediately and acutely conscious of the communal life bearing us on its current, of those creative depths from which the being and work of the community arise, as we are of the form it assumes and the logic that form expresses. A biology and, moreover, an ontology of the community are being disclosed—laws of its physical and mental nature, its organic rhythm and the vital conditions which determine its growth, usages and culture ; the essential significance of its moral phenomena ; the nature of such institutions as the family, the township, the State, law and property.

*　　*　　*　　*　　*

Those revolutionary changes must necessarily have their repercussions in the religious community. The reality of things, the reality of the soul and the reality of God, confront us with a new impressiveness. The religious life alike in its object, content and development is reality ; the relation between the living soul and the living God ; a real life directed towards Him. It is neither mere emotion nor mere theory ; it is imitation, obedience, receiving and giving.[1] In the Youth movement in which the springs of the new age must be sought, the fundamental question is no longer 'Does God exist ?' but 'What is He like ? Where shall I find Him ? How do I

[1] The constant repetition of the idea of 'realisation' in the writings of Newman, who experienced the individualistic crisis so intensely, is most significant. By this he means the transforming of an object from a purely verbal and conceptual entity into an experience, in which it is apprehended as a reality. This will in turn make our lives serious.

stand towards Him ? How can I reach Him ? ' It is not
' Should we pray ? ' but ' How should we pray ? ' not ' Is
asceticism necessary ? ' but ' What kind of asceticism ? '

In this religious relation our fellow men have a vital
part. The religious community exists. Nor is it a collection
of self-contained individuals, but the reality which comprehends individuals—the Church. She embraces the
people ; she embraces mankind. She draws even things,
indeed the whole world, into herself. Thus the Church
is regaining that cosmic spaciousness which was hers
during the early centuries and the Middle Ages. The
conception of the Church as the *Corpus Christi mysticum*,
which is developed in the Epistles of St. Paul to the
Ephesians and Colossians, is acquiring a wholly new
power. Under Christ the Head the Church gathers
together ' all which is in Heaven, on earth, and under the
earth.' In the Church everything—angels, men and
things—are linked with God. In her the great regeneration is already beginning for which the entire creation
' groaneth and is in travail.'

This unity is not a chaotic experience ; it is no mere
outburst of emotion. We are concerned with a community formed and fashioned by dogma, canon law, and
ritual. It is not merely a society, but a religious community ; not a religious movement, but the very life of
the Church ; not a spiritual romanticism, but her existence.

This consciousness of the community is, however,
caught up and permeated by the consciousness of a supernatural life. As in the sphere of natural psychology ' life,'
which is at once so mysterious, yet so completely evident,
is everywhere finding recognition, so it is in the supernatural sphere. Grace is real life ; religious activity is the

development of a higher vitality; the community is participation in a common life, and all forms are forms of life.

And if in the natural sphere we have acquired a clear vision for the structural laws and the organic purpose of life; if we have discovered how one thing fits another, and where man's intellectual objectives lie; if consciousness of the organic is everywhere awakened, the same thing is occurring here. The profound formulas of theology once more reveal their inexhaustible significance for the spiritual life of every day. Our life, whether the life of the individual, or the life of the Church, is 'in Christ, through the Holy Ghost, to the Father.' The Father is the Goal, and to Him the great and final Object, is focussed the vision which alone gives our religion a fixed aim.[1] He is the sublimest and all-embracing sovereign power, and the wisdom which pervades the world, the sublimity which lifts us from narrow ways. The Son is the Way, as He Himself has told us. By His Word, by His life, and by His whole Being He reveals the Father and leads us to Him : 'No man cometh to the Father but by me.' He who acknowledges Christ, he who 'seeth' Him, 'seeth the Father also.' In proportion as we become one with Christ we approach the Father more closely. And the Holy Ghost, the Spirit of Jesus, is the Leader, and shows us the way. He bestows Christ's grace, teaches Christ's truth, and makes Christ's ordinances operative.

---

[1] Because this had been widely forgotten, it was possible for Harnack to present the message of the Father in so one-sided a manner as the content of the work of Christ, that it became, so to speak, coloured with Protestantism. Every page of the Breviary, every prayer of the Mass, loudly proclaims that the aim and aspiration of our whole life is directed to the Father.

This is the law governing the organisation of Christian life
—the law of the Blessed Trinity. Only where order is,
God is. The Father has sent the Son, and He has sent the
Holy Ghost from the Father. In the Church we become
one with the Holy Ghost; He unites us with the Son,
' and he will surely take of his own and give to us.' And
in Christ we come back to the Father.

*   *   *   *   *

An event of tremendous importance has happened.
The religious life no longer rises solely in the self, but at
the same time at the opposite pole, in the objective and
already formed community. There also life originates
and is thus a reciprocal movement between these two
poles. It is once more what of its very nature it should
be, a phenomenon of tension, an arc of flame. And it is
full and free only when its process is an arc rising from
two extremities. The objective is no longer merely the
boundary of the subject to which religion in the strict
sense is confined. It is an essential factor of the religious
life, given from the very outset. It is the presupposition
and content of religion.

The religious life is being released from its fatal confinement within the subject, and draws into itself the entire
fulness of objective reality. As once in the Middle Ages,
all things are re-entering the religious sphere, and moreover with a religious colouring and as religious values.
The rest of mankind and the things of this world once
more are invested with a religious atmosphere and a
profound religious significance. As a result the feeling
for symbolism is coming back; concrete objects once
more become the vehicles and expressions of spiritual

*Cf. Gerald
Vann*

25

reality. We understand how every department of a real world could find a place in the cathedrals of the Middle Ages, in its *Summas*, universal histories, encyclopædias and cycles of legend, and moreover not as an incongruous accessory, not as an allegory stuck on from without, but filled with religious content and itself invested with a spiritual character. Many signs point towards the re-emergence of a religious world. This, however, is the Church, which gathers together under one head ' what is in heaven, on the earth, and under the earth.' The moment seems near for a genuine religious art, which will not be content to depict religious subjects with an unconsecrated brush, but will see the whole world spiritually as a vast kingdom of realities, comprising good and evil powers,[1] and in which the Kingdom of God is taken by storm.

All this, however, can be summed up in one word—' the Church.' That stupendous Fact that is the Church is once more becoming a living reality, and we understand that she truly is the One and the All. We dimly guess something of the passion with which great saints clung to her and fought for her. In the past their words may sometimes have sounded empty phrases. But now a light is breaking ! The thinker, with rapture of spirit, will perceive in the Church the ultimate and vast synthesis of all realities. The artist, with a force that moves his heart to the depths, will experience in the Church the overwhelming transformation, the exquisite refinement, and the sublime transfiguration of all reality by a sovereign

[1] For belief in that which is opposed to God is also religious. Only coldness and intellectual pride are irreligious. He who believes in the devil as a reality, by so doing believes in God also.

radiance and beauty. The man of moral endeavour will see in her the fulness of living perfection, in which all man's capacities are awakened and sanctified in Christ; the power which contrasts uncompromisingly Yea and Nay, and demands a decision between them; the determined fight for God's Kingdom against evil. To the politician—forget, reader, the ugliness which is usually implied by the term; it can bear a noble sense—she is revealed as that supreme order in which every living thing finds its fulfilment and realises the entire significance of its individual being. It achieves this in relation to beings and the whole, and precisely in virtue of its unique individual quality combines with its fellows to build up the great *Civitas*, in which every force and individual peculiarity are alive, but at the same time are disciplined by the vast cosmic order which comes from God, the Three in One. To the man of social temper she offers the experience of an unreserved sharing, in which all belongs to all, and all are one in God, so completely that it would be impossible to conceive a profounder unity.

All this, however, must not be confined to books and speech, but must be put with effect where the Church touches the individual most closely—in the parish. If the process known as the 'Church movement' makes progress, it is bound to lead to a renewal of parochial consciousness. This is the appointed way in which the Church must become an object of personal experience. The measure of the individual's true—not merely verbal—loyalty to the Church lies in the extent to which he lives with her, knows that he is jointly responsible for her, and works for her. And conversely the various manifestations of parish life must in turn be such that the individual is able to behave in this way. Hitherto parish life itself has been deeply tainted by that individualistic spirit of which we have spoken above. How, indeed, could it have been otherwise?

And confirmation is the Sacrament by which the Christian comes into full relation with the Church. By Baptism he becomes a member of the Church, but by Confirmation he becomes one of her citizens, and receives the commission and the power to take to himself the fulness of the Church's life, and himself to exercise—in the degree and manner compatible with his position as a layman—the 'royal priesthood of the holy people.'

* * * * *

It is in the light of what has already been said that we can understand the liturgical movement. This is a particular powerful current and one more exceptionally visible from outside than within the 'Church movement'; indeed, it is the latter in its contemplative aspect. Through it the Church enters the life of prayer as a religious reality, and the life of the individual becomes an integral part of the life of the Church.

Here the individual is as one of the people, not a member of an esoteric group of artists and writers, as, for instance, in the books of J. K. Huysmans, but essentially one of the people. That is to say, he is comprised in the unity which finds room at the same time for the average man and the most extraordinary possibilities of heroism, the unity which comprises both the surface and the deepest roots of humanity, hard, every-day common sense and profound mysticism, which can even include crude popular beliefs which verge on superstition: and which is nevertheless alone competent to judge the realities of life and of the Church because it alone really faces life—its possibilities of development hampered in innumerable respects by poverty and narrow surroundings, and yet, as a whole, the sole complete humanity. The liturgy is essentially not the religion of the cultured, but the religion of the people (cf. p. 19). If the people are rightly instructed, and the liturgy properly carried out, they display a simple and profound understanding of it. For the people do not analyse concepts, but contemplate. The people possess that inner integrity of being which corresponds perfectly with the symbolism of the liturgical language, imagery, action, and ornaments. The cultured man has first of all to accustom himself to this attitude ; but to the people it has always been inconceivable that religion should express itself by abstract ideas and logical developments, and not by being and action, by imagery and ritual.

The liturgy is throughout reality. It is this which distinguishes it from all purely intellectual or emotional piety, from rationalism and religious romanticism. In it man is confronted with physical realities—men, things, ceremonies, ornaments—and with metaphysical realities— a real Christ, real grace. The liturgy is not merely thought, nor is it merely emotion ; it is first and foremost development, growth, ripening, being. The liturgy is a process of fulfilment, a growth to maturity. The whole of nature must be evoked by the liturgy, and as the liturgy seized by grace must take hold of it all, refine and glorify it in the likeness of Christ, through the all-embracing and ardent love of the Holy Ghost for the glory of the Father, whose sovereign Majesty draws all things to Itself.

Thus the liturgy embraces everything in existence,

angels, men and things ; all the content and events of life ; in short, the whole of reality. And natural reality is here made subject to supernatural ; created reality related to the uncreated.

This full reality is shaped by the constructive laws of the Church—by dogma, the law of truth ; by ritual, the law of worship ; and by canon law, the law of order.

The growth itself does not take place according to a programme or regulations carefully thought out, but as all life grows—rhythmically. But we cannot develop this point further now. What proportion and equilibrium are in spatial construction, rhythm is in sequence—systematic repetition in change, so that the following step repeats the previous one, but at the same time goes beyond it. In this way life grows to its fulness and the transformation of the soul is accomplished. The liturgy is a unique rhythm. Incalculable discoveries still await us in this field. What the Middle Ages experienced as a matter of course, what is already contained in the Church's rubrics, but which has vanished from the consciousness of religious people, must be rediscovered.

Its substance, however, is the life of Christ. What He was and did lives again as mystical reality. His life, infused into those rhythms and symbols, is renewed in the changing seasons of the Church's year, and in the perpetual identity of Sacrifice and Sacrament. This process is the organic law by which the believer grows ' unto the measure of the age of the fulness of Christ.' Living by the liturgy does not mean the cultivation of literary tastes and fancies, but self-subjection to the order established by the Holy Ghost Himself ; it means being led by the rule and love of the Holy Ghost to a life in Christ and in Him for the Father.

We have yet to realise what constant discipline, what a profound fashioning, and training of the inner life, this demands. When we do, no one will any longer regard the liturgy as mere æstheticism.

Creation as a whole embraced in the relation with God established by prayer; the fulness of nature, evoked and transfigured by the fulness of grace, organised by the organic law of the Triune God, and steadily growing according to a rhythm perfectly simple yet infinitely rich; the vessel and expression of the life of Christ and the Christian—this is the liturgy. The liturgy is creation, redeemed and at prayer, because it is the Church at prayer.

At Pentecost, when the fulness of the Spirit came upon the Apostles, all those tongues were not sufficient to declare the ' wonderful works of God.'

It often seems as though a breath from that mighty tempest is stirring in our own time ! Our Religion rises before us as a shape so majestic that it leaves us breathless.

But why do I speak of religion ? Did the primitive Christians or the Middle Ages talk about ' Religion ' as we use the word ? Is there such a thing as ' religion ' for the Catholic ? He is a child of the living God, and a member of the living Church.

2

THE CHURCH AND PERSONALITY

If the first lecture has fulfilled its object, it has displayed the spiritual environment in which the Church appears before us to-day. We have seen how as the Church grows in strength a process develops which embraces our entire spiritual life. And now we have to enquire, what is the meaning of this Church, which rises before us in such majesty?

This is the object which we must keep in view. We shall not attempt to prove that the Church is true; we shall take belief in her divinity for granted. But when a scientific investigator has established the existence, in a given part of the body, of a particular organ, formed in a particular manner, he proceeds to investigate its significance for the life of the organism. In the same way we shall seek to discover what is the Church's significance for the religious life as a whole. This is the sense of our question. We shall, it is true, considerably limit the scope of our question. For we shall leave out of account the primary and deepest meaning of the Church, which is that she is God's spiritual universe, His self-revelation and the manifestation of His glory. We shall consider only its other aspect. This concerns the Church in her relation to man's existence and salvation, and her significance for the men who are her members. But we must make a further restriction. We must leave mankind out of account and concentrate wholly upon personality. That is to say, we shall enquire what is the Church's significance for the personal being and life of the man who makes his membership a living reality, for whom the Church is his very life.

*   *   *   *   *

What is the Church? She is the Kingdom of God in mankind. The Kingdom of God—it is the epitome of Christianity. All that Christ was, all that He taught, did, created, and suffered, is contained in these words—He has established the Kingdom of God. The Kingdom of God means that the Creator takes possession of His creature, penetrates it with His light; He fills its will and heart with His own burning love and the root of its being with His own divine peace, and He moulds the entire spirit by the creative power which imposes a new form upon it. The Kingdom of God means that God draws His creature to Himself, and makes it capable of receiving His own fulness; and that He bestows upon it the longing and the power to possess Him. It means—alas, the words are blunted by repetition and our hearts are so dull, or they would catch fire at the thought!—that the boundless fecundity of the divine Love seizes the creature and brings it to that second birth whereby it shares God's own nature and lives with a new life which springs from Himself. In that rebirth the Father makes it His child in Christ Jesus through the Holy Ghost.

This union of man with God is God's Kingdom. In it man belongs to His Creator, and his Creator belongs to Him. Much more of profound significance could be said about this mystery, but we must be content with these few words.

This elevation of the creature is not a natural event but God's free act. It is bound up with the historical personality of Jesus of Nazareth, and with the work which He accomplished at a particular period of history. Nor is it a natural process, but an operation of Grace, exceeding all the forces of nature.

Let us examine it more closely. From the standpoint of God, it is something quite simple. But in the creature it develops to its maturity according to the forms and laws which God has established in the Spirit of man.

God's Kingdom resides in mankind. God takes possession of mankind as such, of the unity, welded by all the biological, geographical, cultural and social ties which bind one human being to others ; that mysterious unity which, though composed entirely of individuals, is more than their sum total. If this whole is to be laid hold upon by God, it is not necessary that all men should be numerically included in it. It is sufficient that God's grace should take hold of the community as such, that something which transcends the individual. This, however, can be accomplished in a small representative group. The little flock at Pentecost was already 'mankind,' because it was an objective community, of which the individual was a member ; it was in a condition to expand, until it slowly included everything, as the mustard seed becomes the tree in which ' the birds of the air . . . dwell.' That is to say we are concerned with a line of force, the direction along which the divine Action operates. God takes possession of men, in so far as a man reaches out above his natural grasp ; inasmuch as men belong to a supra-personal unity, and are, or are capable of becoming, members of a community.

34

In so far, therefore, as God's remodelling and uplifting power is directed towards the community as such, the Church comes into being. The Church is the Kingdom in its supra-personal aspect; the human community, reborn into God's Kingdom. The individual is ' the Church,' in so far as the aim of his life is to assist the building up of the community, and he is a member, a cell of it. This, however, is the case in so far as he is employing those capacities of his being which have a more than merely individual reference and are ordained to the service of the whole, which work for it, give to it and receive from it. The Church is the supra-personal, objective aspect of the Kingdom of God—although of course she consists of individual persons.[1]

The Kingdom of God, however, has a subjective side as well. That is the individual soul, as God's grace takes possession of it in that private and unique individuality by which it exists for itself. The Church embraces a man as he reaches out beyond himself to his fellows, capable and

[1] We must, however, bear in mind the following qualification. What we have said refers solely to that aspect of the Church with which sociology can deal. What the Church is—her actual essence—can never be constructed *a priori*. There is no such thing as a philosophy of the Church, if it is understood to mean more than the consideration of those social phenomena to be found in her, which are also to be found in natural communities, and which reappear in the Church simply because she is a community of human beings. But in the Church these very phenomena differ from their counterparts in all other societies. Even in her natural aspect the Church is unique. And her essence, her distinctively supernatural character is exclusively the effect of a positive work of God, of the historical personality of Christ and her historical institution through Him. Only from revelation can we learn what the Church is in her essence. We can never do more than describe her as that community of faith and grace which Christ founded, and which continues to live on in history as the Catholic Church, with her distinctive and unique character. Only on this presupposition are such books as Pilgram's *Physiologie der Kirche*, or André's *Kirche als Keimzelle der Weltvergöttlichung* valuable, indeed, of very considerable value.

desirous of forming in conjunction with them a community of which he and they are members. The individual personality, however, is also based upon itself, like a globe which revolves around its own axis. And as such, also, God's grace takes possession of it. By this I do not mean that there exists in human beings a sphere which lies outside the Church. That would be too superficial a notion. It is truer to say that the whole man is in the Church, with all that he is. Even in his most individual aspect he is her member, although only in so far as this individuality and its powers are directed to the community. His whole being belongs to it; it is in its social reference—his individuality as related to his fellows and incorporated in the community. But the same individuality has an opposite pole. His powers are also directed inwards to build up a world in which he is alone with himself. In this aspect also he is the subject of God's grace.[1]

For God is the God of mankind as a whole. As such He is concerned with the supra-personal, the community, and its members jointly find in Him the social Deity of which human society has need. But He is also the God of each individual. This is indeed the supreme and fullest revelation of His life—that for each individual He is 'his God.' He is the unique response to the unique need of every individual; possessed by each in the unique manner which his unique personality requires; belonging to him,

---

[1] This is not a contradiction, but a contrast. One term of a contradiction precludes the other—good and bad, yes and no, for example, exclude each other. Every living thing, however, is a unity of contrasts which are differentiated from each other, yet postulate each other. The firm, yet flexible, simple, yet creative, unity of the living organism can only be grasped intellectually as a web of contrasts. I hope to explain this point thoroughly in another book.

as to no other besides, in his unique nature. This is God's Kingdom in the soul, Christian personality.[1]

Clearly this Christian personality is not a sphere lying outside the Church, or something opposed to her, but her organic opposite pole, demanded by her very nature, and yet at the same time determined by her.[2]

We have contrasted the Kingdom of God as the Church with the Kingdom of God as personality. We were obliged to do so, in order to grasp clearly the distinctions between them. But the question at once arises, what is the relation between them ?

We must reply at once and as emphatically as possible : they are not two things separable from each other ; not two ' Kingdoms.' They are aspects of the same basic reality of the Christian life, the same fundamental mystery of grace. There is only one Kingdom of God ; only one divine possession of man by the Father, in Christ, through the Holy Ghost. But it develops along the two fundamental lines of all organic development. And it manifests itself in accordance with the two fundamental modes of

---

[1] This word is not a good one. It is coloured by the associations of individualism, the doctrine of individual autonomy and above all of pure naturalism. St. Paul certainly would not have talked about ' personality.' The notion of Christian personality is as different from its philosophic counterpart as the notion of the ' Church,' Christ's Church, differs from that of the ' Religious Society.' However, I know of no better word ; I use it, therefore, in the sense in which Our Lord speaks of a ' child of God,' and St. Paul, in his Epistles, of the individual Christian as distinct from the community.

[2] This personal sphere has been detached from the religious life as a whole by Protestantism and every other individualistic system and developed in a one-sided manner. Thus the direct communication between God and the redeemed, who is, however, at the same time a member of the Church, was perverted into the autonomy of a completely independent and self-sufficient personality. And the healthy tension of the relationship established by the very nature of its terms was replaced by an unnatural constraint.

37

human nature—in man as he is self-contained and asserts himself as an individual, and in man as he merges in the community which transcends his individuality.

The Kingdom of God is at once the Church and individual personality, and it is both *a priori* and of its very essence. It is definitively the Church; for the Church is the transfiguration of man's nature by grace, so far as he is within the community. It is a kingdom of individual personality in every believer. It is thus both the Church and the individual Christian. They are not independent spheres. Neither can be separated from the other, even if each can be considered separately. On the contrary, of their nature and *a priori* they are interrelated and interdependent.

For the nature of the community as Catholicism understands and realises it, is not such that individual personality has to struggle for self-preservation against it. It is not a power which violates personal individuality, as Communism does, or any other variety of the totalitarian state. On the contrary, Catholic community presupposes from the outset and requires the free individual personalities as its components. In particular the Church is a community of beings, which are not simply members and instruments of the whole, but at the same time are microcosms revolving on their own axes, that is, individual personalities. Mere individuals can constitute only herds or human antheaps; community is a mutual relationship of personalities. This is an ethical requirement, for morality demands a free intercourse. It also results from the very structure of being, for it is only when units with their individual centres, their own *modus operandi* and a life of their own, come together, that there can arise that unity, unique in its tension and flexibility, stable, yet rich in intrinsic possibilities of development, which is termed a community. (See below, pp. 44, 45.)

And Christian personality is not so constituted that it is only as an afterthought associated with others to form a community. Its membership of the community does not originate in a concession made by one individual to another. It is not the case that individuals by nature independent of one another conclude a contract, by which each sacrifices a part of his independence, that by this concession he may save as much of it as possible. That is the view of society held by individualism. Personality as Catholicism understands it, looks in every direction, and thus *a priori* and of its very nature is social, and man's entire being enters into society. A mere sum total of individuals can produce only a crowd. If a large number join together merely by a contract for some definite object, the sole bond which constitutes their society will be this common purpose. A genuine community on the contrary cannot be formed in this way by individuals. It exists from the outset, and is a supra-individual reality, however hard it may be to comprehend from an intellectual conception of its nature.

It is this which fundamentally distinguishes the relationship between the community and the individual as Catholicism understands it from all one-sided conceptions of it, such as Communism and the totalitarian state on the one hand, and individualism or even anarchy on the other. It is not based upon a one-sided psychology or a mental construction, but on reality in its fulness. The Catholic's conception of personality differs from every type of individualism essentially and not merely in degree. For the same individual who is a self-centred unit is at the same time conscious in his whole being, he is a member of the community, in this case of the Church. And in the same way the community is not a mere feeble social restriction or state bondage, but something fundamentally different. It differs as does living being with its innumerable aspects from an artificial construction without flesh and blood. For the community realises that it is made up of individuals, each one of which constitutes a self-contained world and possesses a unique character. This is a fundamental truth which it is most important to understand thoroughly. Unless it is grasped the Catholic view of the Church, indeed of society as such, must be unintelligible. We must not get our sociological principles either from Communism, State Socialism, or individualism. For all these tear the living whole to pieces to exaggerate one portion of it. All are false and diseased. The Catholic conception of society and of individual personality starts on the contrary—like all Catholic teaching—not from isolated axioms or one-sided psychological presuppositions, but from the integrity of real life apprehended without prejudice. In virtue of his nature man is both an individual person and a member of a society. Nor do these two aspects of his being simply co-exist. On the contrary, society exists already as a living seed in man's individuality, and the latter in turn is necessarily presupposed by society as its foundation, though without prejudice to the relative independence of both these two primary forms of human life.

From this point of view also the 'Catholic type of humanity is reappearing at the present day, and shaking off at last the spell of State worship on the one hand, of a disintegrating self-sufficiency on the other. Here, too, we are again handling realities instead of words, and we recognise organic relationships instead of being dominated by abstract conceptions. It is for us to decide whether we shall allow ourselves to be re-enslaved or remain conscious of our mission to be true to the fundamental nature of humanity and express it freely and faithfully in word and deed.

The Church then is a society essentially bound up with individual personality; and the individual life of the Christian is of its very nature related to the community. Both together are required for the perfect realisation of the Kingdom of God. An electric current is impossible, without its two poles. And the one pole cannot exist, or even be conceived, without the other. In the same way the great fundamental Christian reality, the Kingdom of God, is impossible, except as comprising both Church and individual personality, each with its well-defined and distinctive nature, but essentially related to the other. There would be no church if its members were not at the same time mental microcosms, each self-subsistent and alone with God. There would be no Christian personality, if it did not at the same time form part of the community, as its living member. The soul elevated by grace is not something anterior to the Church, as individuals originally isolated formed an alliance. Those who hold this view have failed completely to grasp the essence of Catholic personality. Nor does the Church absorb the individual, so that his personality can be realised only when he wrenches himself free from her. Those who think this do not know what the Church is. When I affirm the ' Church,' I am at the same time affirming individual ' personality,' and when I speak of the interior life of the Christian, I imply the life of the Christian community.

Even now, however, the mutual relationship has not been fully stated. Both the Church and individual personality are necessary. Both, moreover, exist from the first; for neither can be traced back to the other. And if anyone should attempt to ask which of the two is the more valuable in the sight of God, he would see at once that it is a question which cannot be asked. For Christ died for the Church, that He might make her, by His Blood, 'a glorious Church, not having spot or wrinkle.' But He also died for every individual soul. The state in its human weakness sacrifices the individual to the society; God does not. The Church and the individual personality—both, then, are equally primordial, equally essential, equally valuable. Yet there is a profound difference between these two expressions of the Kingdom of God. Priority of rank belongs to the Church. She has authority over the individual. He is subordinated to her: his will to hers, his judgment to hers, and his interests to hers. The Church is invested with the majesty of God, and is the visible representative in face of the individual and the sum total of individuals. She possesses—within the limits imposed by her own nature and the nature of individual personality—the power which God possesses over the creature; she is authority. And, however aware the individual may be of his direct relation to God, and as God's child know that he is emancipated from 'tutors and governors,' and that he enjoys personal communion with God, he is notwithstanding subject to the Church as to God. 'He that heareth you, heareth me.' 'Whatsoever thou shalt bind upon earth, shall be bound also in heaven.'

It is a profound paradox which nevertheless is alone in harmony with the nature of life, and, as soon as the mind's eye is focussed steadily upon it, self-evident.

*   *   *   *   *

From all this one fact emerges. The personal life of the Christian is engaged to its profoundest depth in the Church and affected by her condition. And conversely the Church is to an incalculable degree affected by the spiritual condition of her members. What concerns the Church concerns me. You see at once what this implies. It does not simply mean that a child for instance will be badly taught if the servant of the Church who has charge of his education is inadequate to the task. On the contrary, between the individual and the Church there is an organic solidarity of the most intimate kind. The same Kingdom of God lives in the Church and in the individual Catholic, The state of each is correlative, as the surface of the water is determined by the pipes which supply it. The individual can as little dissociate himself from the state of the Church ; —it would be the illusion of individualism—as the individual cell can dissociate itself from the state of health of the whole body. And conversely it is of a matter of incalculable concern for the Church whether the faithful are men and women of strong and valuable personality, character. The Church could never aim at a power, strength, and depth to be achieved at the expense of the individual personality of her members. For she would imperil the power, strength and depth of her own life. This must not be misunderstood. The Church does not depend for her existence and essential nature upon the spiritual and moral condition of individuals. For, were

43

this the case, she would not be an objective reality. And everything said hitherto has insisted upon her essential objectivity. But in the concrete the abundance and development of her life do depend in every age upon the extent to which her individual members have become what God intended them to be, developed personalities, each unique, with a unique vocation and unique capacities to be fulfilled. The relation between the Church and the individual should never be understood as though either could develop at the expense of the other. This misconception is at the root of the un-Catholic attitude to this question, whether in its Protestant or Byzantine form.

We are Catholic in so far as we grasp—or rather, for this is insufficient—in so far as we live the fact, indeed feel it as obvious in our very bones as something to be taken for granted, that the purity, greatness, and strength of individual personality and of the Church rise and fall together.

*   *   *   *   *

You now realise, I am sure, how very far short of this Catholic frame of mind our ideas are, and even more our deepest and most immediate feelings ; how far the contemporary tension between the community and the individual has affected our view of the relation between the Church and the individual, thereby imperilling its very essence.

We are conscious of a tension between the Church and the individual personality, and the most enthusiastic speeches cannot abolish it. And it is not the tension of which we have already spoken, the tension inherent in the

44

nature of their relationship, which is a source of health and life, but an unnatural and destructive tension. In the Middle Ages the objective reality of the Church, like that of society in general, was directly experienced. The individual had been integrated in the social organism in which he freely developed his distinctive personality. At the Renaissance the individual attained a critical self-consciousness, and asserted his own independence at the expense of the objective community. By so doing, however, he gradually lost sight of his profound dependence upon the entire social organism. Consequently the modern man's consciousness of his own personality is no longer healthy, no longer organically bound up with the conscious life of the community. It has overshot the mark, and detached itself from its organic context. The individual cannot help feeling the Church to be, with her claim to authority, a power hostile to himself. But no hatred pierces deeper than that between complementary forms of life, from which we may form some idea of what this tension involves.

It will be the mission of the coming age once more to envisage truly the relation between the Church and the individual. If this is to be achieved, our conceptions of society and individual personality must once more be adequate. And self-consciousness and the sense of organic life must again be brought into harmony, and the inherent interdependence of the Church and the individual must again be accepted as a self-evident truth. Every age has its special task. And this is equally true of the development of the religious life. To see how the Church and the individual personality are mutually bound together; how they live the one by the other; and how in this mutual relationship we must seek the justification of ecclesiastical authority, and to make this insight once more an integral part of our life and consciousness is the fundamental achievement to which our age is called.

If, however, we wish to succeeed in this task, we must free ourselves from the partial philosophies of the age, such as individualism, State Socialism, or Communism. Once more we must be wholeheartedly Catholic. Our thought and feeling must be determined by the essential nature of the Catholic position, must proceed from that direct insight into the centre of reality which is the privilege of the genuine Catholic.

Individual personality starves in a frigid isolation if it is cut off from the living community, and the Church must necessarily be intolerable to those who fail to see in her the pre-condition of their most individual and personal life ; who view her only as a power which confronts them and which, far from having any share in their most intimate, vital purpose, actually threatens or represses it. Man's living will cannot accept a Church so conceived. He must either rise in revolt against her, or else submit to her as the costly price of salvation. But the man whose eyes have been opened to the meaning of the Church experiences a great and liberating joy. For he sees that she is the living presupposition of his own personal existence, the essential path to his own perfection. And he is aware of profound solidarity between his personal being and the Church ; how the one lives by the other, and how the life of the one is the strength of the other.

That we can love the Church is at once the supreme grace which may be ours to-day, and the grace which we need most. Men and women of the present generation

cannot love the Church merely because they were born
of Catholic parents. We are too conscious of our individual personality. Just as little can that love be produced
by the intoxication of oratory and mass meetings. It is
not only in the sphere of civil life that such drugs have
lost their efficacy. Nor can vague sentiments give us that
love ; our generation is too honest for that. One thing
only can avail—a clear insight into the nature and significance of the Church. We must realise that, as Christians,
our personality is achieved in proportion as we are more
closely incorporated into the Church, and as the Church
lives in us. When we address her, we say with deep
understanding not ' thou ' but ' I.'

If I have really grasped these truths, I shall no longer
regard the Church as a spiritual police force, but blood of
my own blood, the life of whose abundance I live. I shall
see her as the all-embracing Kingdom of my God, and His
Kingdom in my soul as her living counterpart. Then will
she be my Mother and my Queen, the Bride of Christ.
Then I can love her ! And only then can I find peace !

We shall not be at peace with the Church till we
have reached the point at which we can love her. Not till
then . . .

*   *   *   *   *

May these lectures help a little towards this consummation. But I must make one request—do not weigh words !
A particular word or proposition may well be distorted,
and even erroneous. It is not my purpose to offer you
nicely-calculated formulas, but something deeper—trust.
You are, I trust, listening to the underlying meaning I
wish to convey, and that in the light of the whole you will

correct for yourselves any verbal deficiencies or mis-
statements. In short you will, I am sure, make of these
lectures what all speech and hearing, all writing and reading
should be—a joint intellectual creation.

3

THE WAY TO BECOME HUMAN

WE propose to consider the meaning of the Church.
I have already attempted to sketch it in general outline.
For the individual the Church is the living presupposition
of his personal perfection. She is the way to personality.[1]
Before, however, we go into details, allow me to make a
preliminary observation. When I tried to explain the
Church's significance for individual personality, objections, perhaps, came into your minds. Your inner glance
saw many defects confronting it. Your thoughts travelled
back to many personal disillusionments, and therefore you
possibly felt that what I said was untrue. You thought
that what I said was indeed true of the ideal, of a spiritual
church, but that the actual Church is not, and does not
accomplish, what I was maintaining. I owe you an answer
to this objection. Those who could speak of the meaning
of the Church must also speak of her defects. Even the

[1] The way ; that is, an indispensable, but not exclusive way. The
more resolutely an individual acknowledges himself for what he is, and
at the same time endeavours to become and to work out that which God
has destined for him by his individual nature, the more powerfully can
the Church affect him and complete the personality to which she can raise
him. It must once more be repeated that the individualists imagine a
contradiction in this, an ' alternative,' where there is in reality the indispensable pre-condition of organic change. The more unreservedly I
live in the Church, the more completely I shall become that which I
ought to be. I can, however, live in the Church as God, and she herself,
require it, only to the degree in which I mature, awaken to my natural
vocation, and became a self-realising personality. There is a mutual
reciprocity of cause and effect.

Church cannot escape the tragedy inherent in all things human, which arises from the fact that infinite values are bound up with what is human and consequently imperfect. Truth is bound up with human understanding and teaching; the ideal of perfection with its human presentation; the law and form of the community with their human realisation; grace, and even God Himself—remember the Sacrifice of the Mass—bound up with actions performed by men. The Infinitely Perfect blends with the finite and imperfect. This, if we dare say it, is the tragedy of the Eternal Himself, for He must submit Himself to all this if He is to enter the sphere of humanity. And it is the tragedy of man, for he is obliged to accept these human defects, if he would attain the Eternal. All this is as applicable to the Church, as to every institution that exists among human beings. But in her case it has an additional poignancy.

For the highest values are here involved. There is a hierarchy of values, and the higher the value in question, the more painfully will this tragic factor be felt. Here, however, we are concerned with Holiness, with God's Grace and truth, with God Himself. And we are concerned with man's destiny which depends on this Divine Reality—the salvation of his soul. That the State should be well ordered is, of course, of great importance, and so is a well-constructed system of the natural sciences; but in the last resort we can dispense with both. But the values bound up with the Church are as indispensable on the spiritual plane as food in the physical order. Life itself depends upon them. My salvation depends upon God; and I cannot dispense with that. If, however, these supreme values, and consequently the salvation of my soul, are thus intimately bound up with human defects, it will affect me very differently from, for instance, the wrecking of a sound political constitution through party selfishness.

But there is a further consideration. Religion stands in a unique relation to life. When we look more closely, we see that it is itself life ; indeed, it is fundamentally nothing but that abundant life bestowed by God. Its effect, therefore, is to arouse all vital forces and manifestations. As the sun makes plants spring up, so religion awakens life. Within its sphere everything, whether good or bad, is at the highest tension. Goodness is glorified, but evil intensified, if the will does not overcome it. The love of power is oppressive in every sphere, but in the religious most of all. Avarice is always destructive, but when it is found in conjunction with religious values or in a religious context, its effect is peculiarly disastrous. And when sensuality invades religion, it becomes more stifling than anywhere else. If all this is true, the human tragedy is intensified in religion, since any shortcoming is here a heavier burden and more painfully felt.

Yet a further point. In other human institutions the realisation of spiritual values is less rigid. They leave men free to accept or refuse a particular embodiment. The value represented by a well-ordered political system, for instance, is indeed bound up with particular concrete states. But every man is free to abandon any given state and to attach himself to another, whenever he has serious grounds for taking the step. In the Church, however, we must acknowledge not simply the religious value in the abstract, nor the mere fact that it is closely knit with the human element, but that it is bound up with this, and only this particular historic community. The concrete Church, as the embodiment of the religious value, demands our allegiance. And even so, we have not said enough. The truth of Christianity does not consist of abstract tenets and values, which are "attached to the Church." The Truth on which my salvation depends is a Fact, a concrete reality. Christ and the Church are that truth. He said : 'I am the truth.' The Church, however, is His Body. But if the Church is herself Christ, mystically living on, herself the concrete life of truth and the fulness of salvation wrought by the God-man ; and if the values of salvation cannot be detached from her and sought elsewhere, but are once and for all embodied in her as an historical reality, the tragedy will be correspondingly painful, that this dispenser of salvation is so intimately conjoined with human shortcomings.

Therefore, just because the Church is concerned with the supreme values, with the salvation of the soul, because religion focuses the forces of life and thus fosters everything human, both good and bad, because we are here confronted with an historical reality which as such binds us and claims our allegiance, the tragedy of the Church is so intense. So intense is it that we can understand that profound sadness which broods over great spirits. It is the ' *tristezza cosí perenne*,' which is never dispelled on earth, for its source is never dry. Indeed, the purer the soul, the clearer its vision, and the greater its love for the Church, the more profound will that sorrow be.

This tragedy is an integral part of the Church's nature, rooted in her very essence, because ' the Church ' means that God has entered human history ; that Christ, in His nature, power and truth, continues to live in her with a mystical life. It will cease only in Heaven, when the Church militant has become the Church glorified. And even there ? What are we to say of the fact that a particular man who should have become a saint and who could have attained the full possession of God, has not done so ? And who will dare to say that he has fully realised all he might have been ? We are confronted here by one of those ultimate enigmas before which human thought is impotent. Nothing remains but to turn to a Power which is bound by no limits, and whose creative might ' calleth those things that are not, as those that are ' —the Divine Love. Perhaps the tragedy of mankind will prove the opportunity for that love to effect an inconceivable victory in which all human shortcomings will be swallowed up. It has already made it possible for us to call Adam's fault ' blessed.' That the love of God exceeds all bounds and surpasses all justice is the substance of our Christian hope. But for this very reason what we have already said remains true.

To be a Catholic, however, is to accept the Church as she is, together with her tragedy. For the Catholic Christian this acceptance follows from his fundamental assent to the whole of reality. He cannot withdraw into the sphere of pure ideas, feelings, and personal experience. Then, indeed, no ' compromises ' would be any longer required. But the real world would be left to itself, that is, far from God. He may have to bear the reproach that he has fettered the pure Christianity of the Gospel in human power and secular organisation, that he has turned it into a legal religion on the Roman model, a religion of earthly ambitions, has lowered its loftiest standards addressed to a spiritual élite to the capacity of the average man, or however the same charge may be expressed. In fact he has simply been faithful to the stern duty imposed by the real world. He has preferred to renounce a beautiful romanticism of ideals, noble principles and beautiful experiences rather than forget the purpose of Christ—to win reality, with all that the word implies, for the Kingdom of God.

Paradoxical as it may seem, imperfection belongs to the very essence of the Church on earth, the Church as an historical fact. And we may not appeal from the visible Church to the ideal of the Church. We may certainly measure her actual state by what she should become, and may do our best to remove her imperfections. The priest is indeed bound to this task by his ordination, the layman by Confirmation. But we must always accept the real Church as she actually is, place ourselves within her, and make her our starting point.

This, of course, presupposes that we have the courage to endure a state of permanant dissatisfaction. The more deeply a man realises what God is, the loftier his vision of Christ and His Kingdom, the more keenly will he suffer from the imperfection of the Church. That is the profound sorrow which lives in the souls of all great Christians, beneath all the joyousness of a child of God. But the Catholic must not shirk it. There is no place for a Church of æsthetes, an artificial construction of philosophers, or congregation of the millenium. The Church man needs is a church of human beings ; divine, certainly, but including everything that goes to make up humanity, spirit and flesh, indeed earth. For ' the Word was made Flesh,' and the Church is simply Christ, living on, as the content and form of the society He founded. We have, however, the promise that the wheat will never be choked by the tares.

Christ lives on in the Church, but Christ Crucified. One might almost venture to suggest that the defects of the Church are His Cross. The entire Being of the mystical Christ—His truth, His holiness, His grace, and His adorable person—are nailed to them, as once His physical Body to the wood of the Cross. And he who will have Christ, must take His Cross as well. We cannot separate Him from it.

I have already pointed out that we shall only have the right attitude towards the Church's imperfections when we grasp their purpose. It is perhaps this—they are permitted to crucify our faith, so that we may sincerely seek God and our salvation, not ourselves. And that is the reason why they are present in every age. There are those indeed who tell us that the Early Church was ideal. Read the sixth chapter of the Acts of the Apostles. Our Lord had scarcely ascended to Heaven when dissention broke out in the primitive community. And why? The converts from paganism thought that the Jewish Christians received a larger share than they in the distribution of food and money. This surely was a shocking state of affairs? In the community through which the floods of the Spirit still flowed from the Pentecostal outpouring? But everything recorded in Holy Scripture is recorded for a purpose. What should we become if human frailties actually disappeared from the Church? We should probably become proud, selfish and arrogant; æsthetes and reformers of the world. Our belief would no longer spring from the only right motives, to find God and secure eternal happiness for our souls. Instead, we should be Catholics to build up a culture, to enjoy a sublime spirituality, to lead a life full of intellectual beauty. The defects of the Church make any such thing impossible. They are the Cross. They purify our faith.

Moreover, such an attitude is at bottom the only constructive type of criticism, because it is based on affirmation. The man who desires to improve a human being must begin by appreciating him. This preliminary acknowledgment will arouse all his capacities of good and their operation will transform his faults from within. Negative criticism, on the contrary, is content to point out defects. It thus of necessity becomes unjust and puts the person blamed on the defensive. His self-respect and justifiable self-defence ally themselves with his faults and throw their mantle over them. If, however, we begin by accepting the man as a whole and emphasise the good in him, all his capacities of goodness, called forth by love, will be aroused and he will endeavour to become worthy of our approval. The seed has been sown, and a living growth begun which cannot be stayed.

We must, therefore, love the Church as she is. Only so do we truly love her. He alone genuinely loves his friend who loves him as he is, even when he condemns his faults and tries to reform them. In the same way we must accept the Church as she is, and maintain this attitude in everyday life. To be sure we must not let our vision of her failings become obscured, least of all by the artificial enthusiasm aroused by public meetings or newspaper articles. But we must always see through and beyond these defects her essential nature. We must be convinced of her indestructibility and at the same time resolved to do everything that lies in our power, each in his own way and to the extent of his responsibility, to bring her closer to her ideal. This is the Catholic attitude towards the Church.

My introduction has been lengthy. But it was important; so important indeed that I believe that what follows will seem true to you, only in proportion to your agreement with what has been said hitherto.

We saw in the last lecture that the problem we have to face is not the alternative ' the Church or the individual ? ' It concerns rather the relation between these two realities. In theory our aim must be a harmony between the two in which of course the precedence of the Church is fully safeguarded. But the intellectual and spiritual current of a period always flows in a particular direction. Harmonious syntheses are achieved only in brief periods of transition between two different epochs, for example when an age whose outlook is extremely objective and in which the social sense is powerfully developed is yielding to an epoch of individualism. Soon, however, one tendency predominates, and moreover, that which is opposite to the former. The Catholic attitude does not preclude the emphasis being laid on one aspect, otherwise it would be condemned to a monotonous uniformity and would deprive man of history. It demands only that the other aspect shall not be rejected, and coherence with the whole be preserved. That is to say, a particular aspect brought into prominence by the historical situation is emphasised, but is at the same time brought into a vital and organic relationship with the whole. A door is left open to the particular disposition of the historical present, but it is attached to the whole, which always in a sense transcends history. This whole is less actual, but in return it partakes of eternity. It is less progressive, but instead wise, and in the depths is alone in accordance with reality.

Our age is in process of passing from the individualistic and subjective to the social and objective. A stronger emphasis will therefore be laid on the Church. And these lectures will do the same. They will enquire how individual personality, by surrender to the Church, becomes what it should be. My lecture to-day will show how the Church is the way to individual personality. And I shall proceed from the fact that the Church is the spiritual locality where the individual finds himself face to face with the Absolute ; the power that effects and maintains this confrontation.

*   *   *   *   *

Let us try to realise how deeply we are sunk in relativism, that is, the attitude of mind which either denies an Absolute altogether, or at any rate tries to restrict it within the narrowest limits.

We have lived through the collapse of an edifice which we expected to endure for an incalculable period of time, the collapse of the political structure of our country and its power, of the social and economic order existing hitherto, and with it of much besides. We can watch the social sense changing. And our mental attitude towards objects and life in general is equally changing. These changes go too deep to be dismissed with a few words. Artistic vision has changed ; the expressionism, which had gradually become familiar, is already yielding, and the desire is springing up for a new classicism. A scientific and philosophical view of the universe is forming, which strives to attain a loftier and a freer understanding of objects in accordance with their essential nature.

Faced with these profound changes we become rather more acutely conscious of what in truth is always happening—that the attitude of the soul towards itself, its environment, and the first principles of being, is continually shifting. The forms of human life, economic, social, technical, artistic and intellectual, are seen to be in a state of steady, if slight, transformation.

We live in a perpetual flux. As long as this flux is not too clearly perceived, as long as a naive conviction ensures a strong underlying reserve of vitality, or deeply-rooted religious beliefs balance the increase of knowledge, life can endure it.

But in periods of transition, and when centuries of criticism have worn away all fixed belief, the flux forces itself on the mind with an evidence from which there is no escape. The condition ensues which ten years ago was universally predominant, and is still widespread to-day; a sense of transitoriness and limitation takes possession of the soul. It realises with horror how all things are in flux, are passing away. Nothing any longer stands firm. Everything can be viewed from a thousand different angles. What had seemed secure disintegrates, on closer inspection, into a series of probabilities. To every thing produced there are many possible alternatives. Every institution might equally well have been ordered otherwise. Every valuation is only provisional.

Man thus becomes uncertain and vacillating. His judgments are no longer steady, his valuations unhesitating. He is no longer capable of action based on firm conviction and certain of its aim. He is at the mercy of the fashions prevalent in his surroundings, the fluctuations of public opinion, and his own moods. He no longer possesses any dignity. His life drifts. He lacks everything which we mean by character. Such a man is no longer capable of conquest. He cannot overcome error by truth, evil and weakness by moral strength, the stupidity and inconstancy of the masses by great ideas and responsible leadership, or the flux of time by works born of the determination to embody the eternal values.

But this spiritual and intellectual poverty is accompanied by a colossal pride. Man is morbidly uncertain and morbidly arrogant. The nations are confused by pride, parties are blinded by self-seeking, and rich and poor alike are the prey of an ignoble greed. Every social class deifies itself. Art, science, technology—every separate department of life considers itself the sum and substance of reality. There is despairing weakness, hopeless instability, a melancholy consciousness of being at the mercy of a blind irrational force—and side by side with these a pride, as horrible as it is absurd, of money, knowledge, power, and ability.

Impotence and pride, helplessness and arrogance, weakness and violence—do you realise how by the continued action of these vices true humanity has been lost? We are witnessing a caricature of humanity. In what then does humanity in the deepest sense of the term consist? To be truly human is to be conscious of human weakness, but confident that it can be overcome. It is to be humble, but assured. It is to realise man's transience, but aspire to the eternal. It is to be a prisoner of time, but a freeman of eternity. It is to be aware of one's powers, of one's limitations, but to be resolved to accomplish deeds of everlasting worth.

What is a complete humanity ? When neither of these two essential aspects is obscured, but each is asserted and developed ; when they neither destroy each other nor drive each other to extremes, but blend in an evident unity replete with inner tension yet firm, imperilled, yet assured, limited, yet bound on an infinite voyage, this is a complete humanity, And a man is human in so far as he lives, consciously, willingly, and with a cheerful promptitude as a finite being in the midst of time, change, and the countless shapes of life—but at the same time strives to overcome all this flux and limitation in the eternity, and infinity, which transfigure them. A man is human in so far as he truly and humbly combines these two essential aspects. Herein lies the inexpressible charm of all things human—a mystery pregnant with pain and strength, desire and confident hope.

*   *   *   *   *

Well then—the Church is always confronting man with the Reality which creates in him the right attitude of mind : namely, the Absolute.

She confronts him with the Unconditioned. In that encounter he realises that he himself is dependent at every point, but there awakens in him the yearning for a life free from the countless dependencies of life on earth, an existence inwardly full. She confronts him with the Eternal, he realises that he is transitory, but destined to life without end. She confronts him with Infinity, and he realises that he is limited to the very depths of his being, but that the Infinite alone can satisfy him.

The Church continually arouses in him that tension which constitutes the very foundation of his nature : the tension between being and the desire to be, between actuality and a task to be accomplished. And she resolves it for him by the mystery of his likeness to God and of God's love, which bestows of its fulness that which totally surpasses the nature. He is not God, but a creature, yet he is God's image and therefore capable of apprehending and possessing God. *Capax Dei*, as St. Augustine says, able to grasp and hold the Absolute. And God Himself is love. He has made the creature in His own image. It is His will that this resemblance should be perfected by obedience, discipline, and union with Himself. He has redeemed man, and by grace has given him a new birth and made him god-like. But all this means that God has made man for His living kingdom.

But observe this encounter with the Absolute, in which man faces the Infinite and sees clearly what he is, and what It is ; but which at the same time awakens the longing for this Absolute Godhead and the confident expectation of its fulfilment by His love—this fundamental experience of Christianity, truth, humility, yearning love, and confident hope in one, is the moment in which for the first time in the spiritual sense man becomes truly human.

This transformation of a creature into man in the presence of the Absolute is the work of the Church.

*   *   *   *   *

She accomplishes it in various ways. In the first place, through her very existence, through that character which Jesus compared to a rock, the living self-revelation of the eternal God in her.

But in particular there are three essential expressions of the Absolute in the Church—her dogma, her moral and social system, and her liturgy.

The thought of modern man is relativist. He sees that historical fact is at every point conditioned by something other than itself, and everything, therefore, appears subject to change. Experimental research has made him extremely cautious, and he is wary of drawing conclusions. He has become accustomed to critical thinking, and does not readily venture beyond hypotheses and qualified statements. Statistics have taught him conscientious regard for exactitude, and he is apt to demand of any conclusion a complete experimental proof which is unattainable. He has thus become uncertain and hesitant where truth is concerned.

At this point the Church comforts him with dogma. We shall not discuss its detailed content. We are solely concerned with the fact that we are here presented with and apprehend truths unconditionally valid, independently of changing historical conditions, the accuracy of experimental research, and the scruples of methodical criticism. Nor shall we consider the factor of Catholic doctrine which is itself temporally conditioned and therefore changeable. We are dealing only with its unchangeable content, with dogma in the strict sense. He who approaches dogma in the attitude of faith will find in it the Absolute. He thus comes to realise how extremely unreliable is his own knowledge. But he is confronted by Truth divinely guaranteed and unconditional. If he honestly assents to it, he becomes ' human.'

He has a correct valuation of himself. His judgments are clear, free and humble. But at the same time he is aware that there is an Absolute, and that it confronts him here and now in its plenitude. By his faith he receives the Absolute into his soul. Humility and confidence, sincerity and trust unite to constitute the fundamental disposition of a thought adequate with the nature of things. Henceforward the unconditional organises the believer's thought and his entire spiritual life. Man is aware of something, which is absolutely fixed. This becomes the axis upon which his entire mental world turns, a solid core of truth which gives consistency and order to his entire experience. For it becomes the instinctive measure of all his thinking even in the secular sphere, the point of departure for all his intellectual activity. Order is established in his inner life. Those distinctions are grasped without which no intellectual life is possible—the distinction between certainty and uncertainty, truth and error, the great and the petty. The soul becomes calm and joyful, able to acknowledge its limitations yet strive after infinity, to see its dependence, yet overcome it.

This is what is meant by becoming human.

Moral purpose is relative ; ideals of perfection, standards of goodness, and codes of individual and of social behaviour are fluctuating and unstable. Effort is thus crippled, and the will, powerless when important decisions must be made, will in compensation give a free rein to arbitrary impulse in some particular sphere.

The Church confronts man with a world of absolute values, an essential pattern of unconditional perfection, an order of life whose features bear the stamp of truth. It is the Person of Christ. It is the structure of values and standards which He personified and taught, and which lives on in the moral and hierarchical order of the Church.

The effect thus produced is the same, as before, though now in the field of valuations and moral judgment, in the life of practice and production ; man is confronted with what is unconditionally valid. He faces and acknowledges his own essential limitation. But at the same time he sees that he can attach his finite life at every point to God's Infinite Life, and fill it with an unlimited content. He there finds rest. He rejoices in the fact that he is a creature, and still more that he is called to be a ' partaker of the Divine Nature.' His inner life becomes real, concentrated around a fixed centre, supported by eternal laws. His goal becomes clear, his action resolute, his whole life ordered and coherent—he becomes human.

Men envisage their relationship with God in various and shifting fashions. One man beholds God in every object, in tree and stone and sea. To another He speaks from the rigid and sublime laws of thought and duty. A third sees Him as the Great Organiser and Architect. Yet another finds Him in the life of the community, in love and in neighbourly assistance. One man has a clear conception of God ; for another He is a vague entity, the Great Incomprehensible ; to a third He is an abstraction. Indeed the same man may have different conceptions of God according to his age, experience, or moods. The danger thus arises that man may make God in his own image, and so form a finite and petty conception of Him ; that his longing and prayer may no more reach out freely beyond himself, but may degenerate into a dialogue with an enlargement of his own portrait.

In the liturgy the Church displays God as He really is, clearly and unmistakably, in all His greatness, and sets us in His presence as His creatures. She teaches us those aboriginal methods of communion with God which are adapted to His nature and ours—Prayer, Sacrifice, Sacraments. Through sacred actions and readings she awakes in us those great fundamental emotions of adoration, gratitude, penitence and petition.

In the liturgy man stands before God as He really is, in an attitude of prayer which acknowledges that man is a creature and gives honour to God. This brings the entire spiritual world into the right perspective. Everything is called by the right name and assumes its real form—face to face with the true God, man becomes truly man.

*　　　*　　　*　　　*　　　*

That man should see with perfect clearness what he is, a creature; but that he should rejoice in this fact, and regard it as the starting point of his ascent to the Divine, that he should be humble, but strive after the highest; sincere, but full of confidence, and so for the first time be truly human; is the work of the Church. She tells man everywhere, ' Thou art but a creature, yet made in God's image, and God is Love. Therefore He will be thine, if only thou dost will it.'

4

THE ROAD TO FREEDOM

WHEN the Catholic Christian handles a vital issue theoretically or practically, the situation should be immediately altered. It should be as when something is brought out from a false light into the full and clear light of day; or an object previously held in the violent grasp of some boorish bully has been released from his possession and passes into the hands of one who can respect and appreciate it. Every object brought into the Catholic sphere of influence and subjected to the Catholic spirit should recover its freedom and once more fully realise its nature. The Catholic spirit should impose the true standard, the great should appear great, and the petty, petty; and light and shadow put in the right place. . . . Yes—so it would be if one were really Catholic! Then indeed we should possess that true Goodness which sees all things as they are, and brings freedom. And life, which everywhere is suffering violence, would again breathe freely in all that we are and do, and all things be made new!

This is certainly expected of the Catholic Christian by those who are looking on at him from without. They do not expect him to talk brilliantly, or to live in an exceptional fashion remote from life, arbitrary and one-sided. There is an intelligentsia which in an intellectual fashion does violence to life more brilliantly and more significantly than he. These onlookers do not expect this from the

Catholic. They expect him to possess something of Adam's pure vision, and that creative power with which the first man named all things according to their nature. They expect to find in him a glance which proceeds from the centre of the soul and penetrates the heart of objects, and to which they reveal themselves completely; that great love which redeems the silent misery of the world.[1]

But we are not really Catholic, if the term is to be understood in its full and exacting implication, and it is our great, if painful, good fortune that we realise how little we are Catholic. But to be truly Catholic is the real, indeed the only genuine form of human existence, its way of life dictated at once by man's deepest nature and by divine revelation. It is a way of looking at things and of thinking about them which becomes instinctive. This, however, can be formed only in the operation of a long tradition, when the personal attitude of individuals has taken shape in objective forms, customs, organisations, practical achievements, and these exert a formative influence upon individuals, to be in turn remoulded by them. The Reformation and the *Aufklärung* have wrought incalcu-

---

[1] I do not think that I am exaggerating the case. What else are those numerous men and women seeking in the Church, who are looking towards her to-day? No doubt some may be influenced by a romantic preciosity; others, by the desire to find something solid in whatever quarter, without any genuine conviction that here, and here alone, truth is to be found; and fashion also plays its part, as in the interest in Buddhism or primitive cultures. This cannot be denied. But there is more than this. We can detect the expectation that in Catholicism the Essential —the Eternal, the Absolute—finds its due recognition. The man of to-day expects to find a substantial piety in the Church, independent of time, place or fashion, reality—of being and conduct—in every department of life. And it will be a bitter disappointment for which we shall all be jointly responsible, if this expectation is disappointed, not by the Church, but by her members.

lable destruction ; we are all under the influence of the individualistic, naturalistic, and liberal spirit.

We are, therefore, no doubt taking a risk when we speak about human life, without being really Catholic. But we do it tentatively, and well aware that the greatest merit we can achieve is to be forerunners. Our master is St. John the Baptist, who said that after him One was to come Whom the Holy Spirit would baptise with fire. It is only after us that there will come those who will think, feel, produce and speak, out of the fulness of Catholic life. Ours must be the meagre joy of being allowed to prepare their way.

*   *   *   *   *

We are going to speak about one of the supreme treasures of life—about freedom.

How shop-soiled this word has become, and yet it is one of the most noble ! How often have we Catholics allowed the most intimate of our possessions to be taken from us ; and filled with the spirit of error, and then listen suspiciously to what our soul should utter with the deep accents of her native speech ! Freedom—what a dubious connotation the word has acquired ! Yet it contains the sum of what Christ has brought us. It is one of those royal words with which the spiritual masters of the Middle Ages described the majesty of God. ' God the free,' they called Him.

*   *   *   *   *

What then is freedom ? What sort of man, exactly, is the free man ?

To answer that freedom is the absence of external constraint, the power to choose, according to one's own will, among several possible courses, gives no notion of the wealth comprised in the term. For it cannot be contained in a short phrase.

Let us try to bring to light something of this treasure.

Each one of us possesses a pattern of his being, the divine idea, in which the Creator contemplated him. It comprises not only the universal idea of human nature, but everything besides, which constitutes this particular individual. Every individual is unique, and a unique variety of human nature. Indeed, the Rembrandt-German [1] could say truly, could even maintain, strictly speaking, that a number of people should not be counted together, because in reality each is unique, and cannot be compared with the rest.

When this unique quality of a man's individual being is allowed to emerge, and determines all his existence and activities; when he lives from the centre of his own being, not, however, putting an artificial restraint upon himself, but naturally and as a matter of course, he is a free man. He is free who lives in complete harmony with the divine idea of his personality, and who is what his Creator willed him to be. He has achieved a complete equilibrium, the effect of a tension but a resolved tension, a powerful yet gentle rhythm of life, a life at once rich and concentrated, full yet restrained.

All this, however, is but a part of true freedom. The free man must also see things as they are, with a vision not

---

[1] Julius Langbehn, 1851–1907. He became famous as a result of his book *Rembrandt als Erzieher*, published in 1890. This work is a criticism of German pre-war culture, which Langbehn viewed as heading for disaster. At the same time it sets forth his belief in the passing of the ' age of paper ' into a new ' age of art,' which was to be brought about through the primary forces inherent in the German people. Langbehn was received into the Church in 1900. (Translator's Note.)

clouded by mistrust, nor narrowed by prejudice, nor distorted by passion, whether hatred, pride, or selfishness ;
must see them in the fulness of their objective reality, and
in their genuine measure. He must see them in their
entirety, rounded off, displayed on all sides, in their true
relations with other objects, and in their right order. He
will thus see them from the standpoint of their divine idea,
just as they are. His glance will pierce from the centre of
his soul to the centre of its objects. His love, issuing from
an entire heart, will embrace their entire fulness. And his
action, supported by a personality not divided against
itself, grasps the world steadily and draws from it that
which had awaited the hand of God's child, to be brought
pure and complete into the light.

That man should respond to the true nature of things
with the integrity of his own nature and in the unique
fashion of his divinely ordained individuality, that the
divine idea within and that without encounter each other
in his personal life—this is freedom.

*   *   *   *   *

But freedom is even more than this. A man is free
when he can see the great as great, and the small as small ;
the worthless as worthless and the valuable as valuable ;
when he views correctly the distinctions between different
objects and different conditions ; the relations between
objects and their measure. He is free when he recognises
honestly the hierarchy of objects, and their values, placing
its base and its apex, and each intermediate point in its
right position. He is free when he apprehends the idea in
its purity, but contemplates in its light the complete
reality ; when he sees everyday life with all its rough and

tumble and all its shortcomings, but also what is eternal in it. He is free when his vision of the idea does not blind him to reality, and everyday existence does not make him oblivious of the idea, when he ' can gaze upon the stars, but find his way through the streets.'

To see all this, to hold fast to the vision with stout heart and unswerving will, and act in accordance with it amid the confusion of appearances and passions—this is freedom.

But he must do this not because a compulsion is upon him, but because he himself is resolved upon it; not merely as the laborious and painful application of principles, but because the impulse and volition of his own nature impel him, and because the very heart of his personality is thereby fulfilled—thus and not otherwise is he free.

Freedom is a great thing—the supreme fulfilment and the purest standard of worth, truth and peace.

And with all that we have said we still have not plumbed the ultimate depth of freedom. It is that the man who is truly free is open to God and plunged in Him. This is freedom for God and in God.

You will ask, if that is freedom, are we free? Outwardly, of course, we are often free. We can resist a palpable restraint. Psychologically also, for we can choose between right and left. But freedom in the comprehensive sense which we have given? No, we must certainly acknowledge that we are slaves.

Here once more we encounter the mission of the Church —she, and she alone, conducts us to this freedom.

* * * * *

What are the bonds which a man must break to win this complete freedom?

There are in the first place those external circumstances which impede a man's development. These can be very strong; but if his energy is sufficient, he will in the end overcome them, either outwardly, by altering them, or inwardly, by a free renunciation which raises him above them.

The intellectual environment binds more potently, through current opinions, customs and tradition; through all those imponderable but constantly operative forces of example and of influence, mental and emotional. These things penetrate to the profoundest depths of the spirit. Even genius cannot wholly break their spells. And we average people are all subject to these influences, whether we consent to them or oppose them.

Just consider for a moment the extent of their sway. What cannot be effected by a slogan if the environment is favourable? No one can altogether escape its power. How powerful are the intellectual tendencies of an epoch! So potent can they be that ideas which are simply incomprehensible when the intellectual situation has changed may receive the unquestioning credence due to dogmas of faith. Do we not ask ourselves with amazement to-day how certain ideas of Kant's could have been accepted as so many dogmas, disagreement with them regarded as a proof of intellectual weakness? Remember, too, how powerful a compulsion is exercised by highly developed forms of art if the cultural environment is congenial. Think of the manifold ways, often so subtle as to defy discovery, in which certain political, social, or economic forms, for example, democracy or capitalism, mould a man's entire psychology; how a type of humanity recognised as ideal, for example, the knight, the monk, or the traveller, shapes men by its influence to the very core of their being. Against such forces the individual is powerless.

Reflect how, under the spell of such a general tendency, a particular age, the Renaissance, for example, with the decision born of the sense of an immeasurable superiority, rejects what another age—in this case the Middle Ages—had ardently embraced, how we are only now beginning to regard the Renaissance and what followed it as a disaster, and the Middle Ages as—rightly understood—our future. And bear in mind that this was no mere change of externals, but of man's attitude to essentials, values and ideas. In view of all this we have only one choice. Either we must canonize relativism in one shape or another, whether in its cruder form, the doctrine of the milieu, or in the form given to it by Keyserling, psychologically more profound and resting on a metaphysical basis, or embrace with our whole soul a power which can emancipate us.

It is the Church.

*   *   *   *   *

In the Church eternity enters time. Even in the Church, it is true, there is much which is temporal. No one acquainted with her history will deny it. But the substance of her doctrine, the fundamental facts which determine the structure of her religious system and the general outlines of her moral code and her ideal of perfection, transcend time.

In the first place, of her very nature she thinks with the

mind, not of any one race, but of the entire and Catholic world. She judges and lives, not by the insight of the passing moment, but by tradition. The latter, however, is the sum total of the collective experience of her past. She thus transcends local, national and temporal limitations, and those who live and think with her have a *point d'appui* above all such restricted fields of vision, and can therefore attain a freer outlook.

The Church of her nature is rooted, not in particular local conditions or particular historical periods, but in the sphere above space and time, in the eternally abiding. She enters, of course, into relation with every age. But she also opposes each. The Church is never modern. This was the case even in the Middle Ages. We have only to read between the lines of the *Imitation* to detect it. The present always reproaches the Church with belonging to the past. But this is a misconception; the truth is that the Church does not belong to time. She is inwardly detached from everything temporal, and is even somewhat sceptical in her attitude to it.

And she has also had to endure the constant charge that she is not national, that she represents foreign nations, not the particular nation in question. It is a misconception of the truth. In the last resort she is not concerned with nations, but with humanity as a whole, and individual men and women. These, however, are the two expressions of humanity which touch eternity, while everything lying between them, and in particular political and national organisations, are bound to time.

The Church, therefore, stands amid the currents of intellectual fashion like a vast breakwater. She is the power which resists the spell of every historical movement,

no matter what. She opposes the strength of her mis-
givings to every force which threatens to enslave the soul
—economic theories, political slogans, human ideals of
perfection, psychological fashions—and repudiates their
claim to absolute validity. The Church is always the
opponent of the contemporary. When an idea is new, it
exercises a special attraction. It is fresh and novel ; opens
up to the mind unexplored avenues of thought, and thus
arouses far more enthusiasm than its intrinsic value merits.
And when a people becomes acquainted with a culture
previously unknown and the conditions are favourable, it
takes an irresistible hold upon that people, as Asiatic
culture, for example, is affecting us to-day. In the same
way new tendencies in art, new political principles, indeed
novelties in every sphere down to such externals as
fashions of dress and the conventions of social intercourse.
If the environment is receptive, everything new is doubly
potent, like oxygen *in statu nascendi*. Very often its power
bears hardly any proportion to its true value, with the
result that our picture of it is falsified to the point of dis-
tortion. The present, therefore, is always to a certain
extent an hallucination and a prison. It has always
attacked the Church, because it is over-excited, and her
timeless calm resists its petulant importunacy ; because it
is one-sided, and her comprehensiveness transcends its
limited vision. And the Church has always been the foe
of the present, because its unspiritual violence enslaves the
soul and its obtrusive clamour drowns the voice of
eternity. In every age the Church opposes what is Here
and Now for the sake of For Ever ; the contemporary
tendencies and ' politics,' for the sake of those aspects of
humanity which are open to eternity—individual per-

sonality and mankind. When this has been understood, a great deal becomes clear.

He who lives with the Church will experience at first an impatient resentment, because she is constantly bidding him to oppose the aims of his contemporaries. So long as he regards what is being said everywhere, the public opinion prevalent at the moment, as the last word on any question, and makes parties or nations his criteria of value, he will inevitably feel himself condemned to obscurantism. But once the bandage has been removed from his eyes, he will acknowledge that the Church always releases those who live in her from the tyranny of the temporal, and to measure its values gives him the standard of abiding truth. It is a remarkable fact that no one is more sceptical, more inwardly independent of ' what everyone says ' than the man who really lives in the Church. And as a man abandons his union with her, to the same degree does he succumb to the powerful illusions of his environment, even to the extent of sheer superstition. And surely the decision between those two attitudes involves the very roots of human culture. The Church is indeed the road to freedom.

* * * * *

But we have not spoken so far of the strongest bonds of all, those imposed by a man's own character.

There are, in the first place, psychological characteristics common to all men as such, passions, for example, and tendencies of the will. Only if we could conceive knowledge as the purely logical operations of a purely logical subject, as a kind of intellectual mechanism, which always functions smoothly, and which can immediately be set in motion under any conditions, would it be possible to regard it as unaffected by the other psychological functions. But the subject of thought is not an abstract, logical subject, but a living man ; thought is a vitally real relation between man and the object of his thought. In the function of thinking all his other activities and states participate, fatigue, for example, and energy strung to the tensest pitch, joy and depression, success and failure. The experience of every day proves that our intellectual productivity, the direction of our thoughts and the nature of our conclusions, are influenced by the vicissitudes of daily life. Our psychological states may assist, hamper or completely prevent acts of knowledge, strengthen or weaken the persuasiveness of arguments. Desire, love, anger, a longing for revenge, gratitude—anyone who is honest with himself must admit how enormously the force of an argument, apparently purely logical, fluctuates in accordance with his prevalent mood, or the person who puts it forward. Even the climax of the cognitive process —the evidence, the subjective certainty of a judgment, a conclusion, a structure of reasoning—is to an enormous extent subject, as you can see for yourselves, to the influence of psychological states and the external environment. It is a strange chapter in practical epistemology.

So far we have been speaking only of speculative thought. There remains the whole order of values, judgments, pronouncements about good and evil, the lawful and the unlawful, the honourable and the dishonourable, the valuable, the less valuable, and the worthless. How enormously these judgments depend on the fact that the man who forms them acknowledges, esteems, and loves the value in question, or rejects, hates and despises, and on his general attitude towards men and things ; whether he is receptive or self-contained, trustful or suspicious, has keener eyes for good or evil.

When you reflect upon all this, you must admit that our thought and valuations are permeated to the depths by the influences of a man's personal characteristics, his stage of development, and his experiences.

By this I do not mean that our thought and judgments are merely a product of our internal and external conditions ; no reduction of thought and valuation to psychological and sociological processes is implied. Their nucleus is intellectual, but it is embedded in those processes. Thought has an objective reference, and is always striving to realise it more purely, that is to say, to grasp more perfectly objective truth. It has an objective content, this very truth—and becomes more perfect as this content becomes richer and more distinct. In spite of this, however, thought is life, and valuation is life—a vitally real relation between man and the object. And everything which affects that man or the object plays its part in the process.

What will bring us release from this imprisonment ? Most certainly no philosophy ; no self-training, no culture. Man can be set free only by a power that opens his eyes to his own inner dependence and raises him above it, a power that speaks from the eternal, independent at its centre of all these trammels. It must hold up unswervingly to men the ultimate truths, the final picture of perfection, and the deepest standards of value, and must not allow itself to be led astray by any passion, by any fluctuations of sentiment, or by any deceits of self-seeking.

This power is the Church. As contrasted with the

individual soul she may easily give an impression of coldness and rigidity. But to the man who has grasped her essence, she becomes pure life. Certainly it is a life so abundant that the weakly, irritable man of to-day cannot easily experience it. The Church clears the path to freedom through the trammels of environment and individual psychology. In spite of all her shortcomings, she shows man truth seen in its essence, and a pure image of perfection adapted to his nature.

He is thus enabled to escape his personal bondage.

*   *   *   *   *

Once more we must delve deeper, and at last we shall reach our conclusion.

We have spoken of the inner pattern contained in every individual personality which determines its unique quality. The individual is not a human being in general, but bears a stamp peculiar to himself. He embodies a distinctive form in virtue of which he realises human nature in a special way. It is the organic ideal and fundamental law of his entire being and activity. It is expressed in everything he is or does ; it determines his disposition and external attitude. It is, however, the task of the individual—we shall return to this point later—to acknowledge this individual form, bring it out, see its limitations, and place it in its due relation to the world as a whole. The strength of the individual lies in this unique quality. It represents what God desires him to be, his mission and his task. But at the same time it is the source of his weakness.

Consider first those more general mental types which classify men into distinct groups, that is to say, fundamental types of character. Thought is determined by them, the way in which things are seen, will and emotion, and the attitude towards self, man, the world, and God.

We shall sketch one example of these types of character, though only in general outline. We shall call it the synthetic type. A man of this type is interested in similarity and combination. This is already evident in his own nature. There thought, will, activity and emotion strongly tend towards unity and effect a thoroughgoing harmony. Such a man gets quickly into touch with things, and can easily pass from one to another. In objects he sees first of all their similarities, the connecting links and numerous transitions between them. He is powerfully aware of their unity, and if he gives a free rein to his native temper he will reach some type of monism, that is to say, a conception of the universe based wholly on the tendency to likeness and unity which pervades reality. He is, of course, aware of the distinctions between things, but regards them as of secondary importance and is disposed to relegate them increasingly to the background and to explain them away as mere stages of development, transitional forms, and modes of the one great unity. He will even by degrees transform the relation between God and the universe into a unity, and regard Him as simply the Energy at work in all things, maintaining and animating them. And his practice will correspond with his thought. His fundamental attitude will be one of conciliation unless, indeed, as a result of the law of psychological ambivalence, he develops a passionate antagonism towards external objects, which, however, is at bottom determined by his sense of affinity with them. In every sphere he seeks a compromise. He explains evil as due to accidental imperfections, or as a necessary step in the development of good. Thus in practice and theory he is a monist, though his monism may wear a rationalist, æsthetic or religious colour.

A man of this type proves and disproves, unaware of the extent to which he is in the power of his own disposition. He persistently selects from reality those features which suit his nature, and passes over or distorts those which are opposed to it. In the last resort his entire view of the world is an attempt to establish his personal preference by rational proofs.

The opposite temper may express itself similarly. It gives birth to that fundamentally critical attitude which in any sphere notices past and present unlikenesses, what differentiates one object from another, their limitations and dividing lines. For men of this type the world is dissolved into isolated units. The distinctive qualities of objects stand out sharply side by side ; the classifications made by thought are not linked up with sensation and desire. The distinctions between what is and what ought to be, between duty and right, and moral choices stand out rigid and inexorable. Conflicts, the decision between alternatives, are universal.

If this type of man follows his bent to the full, he also is enslaved. He, also, chooses, values, and measures in accordance with ' his own mind,' and is convinced that the result is objective truth. When the intellectual processes of a mind dominated by its period are listed in the light of their psychological presuppositions, the effect is peculiarly devastating. A host of affirmations, chains of reasoning and systems of valuations, apparently purely rational, prove but the slightly veiled expression of a particular psychological temperament. One of the most striking instances of this is Kant. His writings develop a system of thought at first sight as purely objective as could be conceived. But simultaneously they reveal their author's most intimate personality. To us, whose mentality is so utterly different, this latter aspect stands out clearly, like the original writing of a restored palimpsest, and we cannot understand how a philosophy so largely the self-expression of a genius could be mistaken for a discovery of the fundamental nature of objective reality. But unless some higher source of truth safeguards us against the danger, we shall inevitably yield credence to some other teacher who proclaims as objective truth what is but the expression of his own mentality, or formulate as serious fact, and with a great display of reasoning, matters which we have devised to express our personal attitude to life.

To return to the two types we described above—neither is free. First and foremost both are slaves as men, as human types. For there exists in every human being, side by side with his predominant mentality, its opposite. Therefore, the synthetic type of mind is also capable of criticism, and the critical type is not devoid of the power of synthesis. But in each case the complementary disposition is weaker; the mentality takes its character from the predominant tendency. But every living organism is subject to a law we may term the economy of force. It tends to use those organs which are particularly developed, so that the rest become increasingly atrophied. Each type, therefore, should develop its complementary aspect to the utmost of its power. Only by this mutual balance it will achieve complete and harmonious development. But the man who is left to himself develops one-sidedly. The predominant trait of his inner psychological composition increasingly asserts itself and thrusts the rest into the background. Over-developed in one direction he is stunted in another. Such a nature, however, is an enslaved nature, for only a being which has developed freely and harmoniously all its native capacities is free.

Moreover, a man whose development is thus one-sided is not free in relation to his environment. For of the rich abundance of its concrete reality he can see only one aspect—that aspect which is adapted to his particular temperament, and for which the powers he has specially fostered have given him a peculiarly acute vision and comprehension. He is thus held captive by it, and incapable of taking an all-round view of reality.

Such men do not live with their full nature, nor in accordance with the idea of their personality, which, whatever its particular emphasis, is always a whole, but merely with a fragment of their true selves. And their life is not in contact with objects as concrete wholes, but merely with artificial selections from them. Each, how-ever, by a singular delusion, maintains that he is complete and his attitude the right one, his impoverished and mutilated world God's free world of full reality.

There are other types and corresponding ways of regarding the world. Each is a power, each the way to a distinctive outlook. But each is also a net liable to entangle the man who casts it. The different types mingle, and the degree of their combination varies. Their energy, warmth and wealth vary. To these must be added national, local and vocational characteristics, and those derived from heredity or environment. And finally, there are those enigmatic qualities which may be said to constitute the colouring, idiosyncrasy or mannerism of the individual, that wholly unique something which belongs to the one individual alone. All these blend with his fundamental type and foster its independent development.

Remember, also, that the instincts of self-preservation, self-love, and the sense of honour, feed a man's predominant disposition, that all his personal experiences are viewed in its light and adjusted to it. You will now be able to gauge its strength.

How then can a man thus in bondage to his disposition be set free?

He must acknowledge, and to the very core of his being, that reality includes all its possible aspects, is all-round. He must recognise that this reality can be grasped only by a subject equally comprehensive in his knowledge, his valuations and his activities; and that he himself does not possess this comprehensiveness, but is fragmentary, the realisation of one possibility of human nature among a host of others. He must recognise the errors which this one-sidedness produces, and how they narrow the outlook and distort the judgment.

He must indeed fully accept his own special disposition, for his nature and his work are based upon it. But he must also fit it into the entire scheme of things. He must correct his own vision of the world by the knowledge of others, complete his own insights by those of other men, and thus stretch out beyond himself to the whole of reality; and this not only in his knowledge, but in his judgments of value and practical conduct.

That is to say, he must not efface his distinctive character and attempt to make his life a patchwork externally sewn together. His distinctive character must always remain the foundation. But character must become vocation, a mission to accomplish a particular work, but within an organic whole and in vital relation to it. Then one-sidedness will become fruitful distinction, bondage be replaced by a free and conscious mission, obstinate self-assertion by a steadfastness in that position within the whole which a man recognises to be his appointed place.

Anyone who honestly attempts this task quickly realises that he cannot accomplish it by himself. Then is the moment of decision. Will he abandon the attempt ? Will he acquiesce in the impossibility ? Will he become a sceptic ? Or will he arrogantly endeavour to make his inner impotence tolerable by declaring it the only right attitude ? In either case, he remains the slave of his own inner bonds, in the deepest sense a Philistine, however eloquent the language with which he proclaims his servitude. Or else his determination to possess truth, reality, the whole, is ready for the sacrifice which alone will lay the way open, ready ' to lose his soul, in order to save it.' If this is his disposition, he will experience the Church as the road to freedom.

Of her nature the Church is beyond and above these bonds, and he who ' surrenders his soul to her, in her shall win it back,' but free, emancipated from its original narrowness, made free of reality as a whole.

*   *   *   *   *

The Church is the whole of reality, seen, valued, and experienced by the entire man. She is co-extensive with being as a whole, and includes the great and the small, the depths and the surfaces, the sublime and the paltry, might and impotence, the extraordinary and the commonplace, harmony and discord. All its values are known, acknowledged, valued and experienced in their degree and this not from the standpoint of any particular type or group, but of humanity as a whole.

The whole of reality, experienced and mastered by the whole of humanity—such, from our present standpoint, is the Church.

The problems with which we are faced here involve experience as a whole. No part of it may be detached from the whole. Every partial question can be correctly envisaged only from the standpoint of the whole, and the whole only in the light of a full personal experience. For this, however, a subject is required which itself is a whole, and this is the Church. She is the one living organism which is not one-sided in its essential nature. Her long history has made her the repository of the entire experience of mankind. Because she is too great to be national her life embraces the whole of humanity. In her men of diverse races, ages, and characters think and live. Every social class, every profession and every personal endowment contribute to her vision of the whole truth, her correct understanding of the structure of human life. All the stages of moral and religious perfection are represented in the Church up to the summits of holiness. And all this fulness of life has been moulded into a tradition, has become an organic unity. Superficialities are subordinated to deeper realities ; intermediate values take precedence of the trifling and the accidental. The fundamental questions of man's attitude to life have been the meditation of centuries ; so that the entire domain of human experience has been covered and the solution of its problems matured. Institutions have had to be maintained through vicissitudes of period and civilisation, and have reached a classical perfection. Consequently, even from the purely natural point of view, the Church represents an organic structure of knowledge, valuation and life, of the most powerful description. To this we must add her supernatural aspect. The Holy Ghost is at work in the Church, raising her consistently above the limits of the merely human. Of Him it is said that He ' searcheth all things.' He is alone the Spirit of discipline and abundant life. To Him ' all things are given.' He is enlightenment and Love. He awakens love, and love alone sees things as they are. He ' sets in order charity ' and causes it to become truth with a clear vision of Christ and His Kingdom. He makes us ' speak the truth in love.' Thus the Church is sovereign above man and above the world, and can do full justice to both.

Dogma that is revealed and supernatural truth binding our assent, is the living expression of this living organism. The entire body of religious truth which it records is seen by a complete man. And it determines the attitude towards truth of the individual Catholic.

And that form of religion in which the entire man enters into a supernatural communion with God—namely, the liturgy—is another living expression of this living organism. It determines the Catholic attitude towards religion in the stricter sense.

Finally, the Church's discipline and constitution—her moral law and ideal of perfection—are yet another living expression of this organism. They determine the Catholic attitude towards ethics.

The Church holds up before man this truth, this scale of values, and this ideal of perfection ; and not as merely possible or advisable, but as obligatory. She calls upon man to rise above his narrowness and grow up to this complete truth, this comprehensive ideal and universal rule of life. She commands it, and disobedience is sin. Only thus does the demand receive sufficient weight to counterbalance human selfishness, with its exaggerated and tenacious self-assertion.

If man obeys and accepts the fundamental sacrifice of self-surrender and trusts himself to the Church; if he extends his ideas to the universal scope of Catholic dogma, enriches his religious sentiment and life by the wealth of the Church's prayer, strives to bring his conduct into conformity with the lofty, complete pattern of perfection, a pattern, moreover, which moulds the private life of the spirit presented by her communal life and her constitution, then he grows in freedom. He grows into the whole, without abandoning what is distinctively his own. On the contrary, for the first time he sees his individuality clearly when it is confronted with all the other human possibilities to be found in the Church. He sees its true significance to be a member of the whole. He perceives it as a vocation, a God-given task, the contribution made possible by his unique character as an individual, which he has to make towards the great common task of life and production.

Thus man develops into a personality. It is rooted in his individuality, but essentially related to the whole. It involves an individual outlook, the consequence of its uniqueness, but this individual outlook is harmonised at every point with the outlook of others because it never loses sight of the whole. It involves also a joyful determination to realise its own nature, but within the framework of the entire organism. Thus the outlook of the genuine personality is comprehensive and recognises other men's points of view. He divines their meaning, and views his own vocation in relation to the whole. Such a man will not display instant enmity towards a personality of different type to his own, as one species of animals is hostile to another. On the contrary, he will co-ordinate both within the superior unity to which both belong, in the performance of a common task in which each supplements the other. He evinces that great power of acceptance which finds room for other types, and is therefore able to share their life. Thus his wealth increases, for what belongs to others is also his.

My attention has been drawn to a saying of St. Paul's in which the Christian's consciousness of this supreme freedom of his entire being finds striking expression: ' The spiritual man judgeth all things : and he himself is judged of no man.' (1 Cor. ii. 15.) The true Christian is sovereign. He possesses a majesty and a freedom which remove him from the jurisdiction of the unbeliever. He cannot on principle be subject to his judgment, since the unbeliever cannot focus the Christian within his field of vision. The vision of the former, on the contrary, embraces ' all things,' and his standard is absolute. How remote is the impoverished consciousness of our Catholicity from this attitude of St. Paul, in which perfect humility—all his Epistles reveal it—is united with the knowledge that he possesses, not one point of view among others, but the unique and absolute point of view ; genuine humility combined with the sublime consciousness of absolute and perfect supremacy.

This is the meaning of ' *sentire cum Ecclesia* '—the way from one-sidedness to completeness, from bondage to freedom, from mere individuality to personality.

Man is truly free in proportion as he is Catholic. But he is Catholic to the extent that he lives, not within the narrow confinement of his purely individual and separate existence, but in the fulness and integrity of the Church, to the extent, that is to say, that he has himself become identified with ' the Church.'

5

COMMUNITY

IDEAS have their seasons, as plants have their seasons of growth, flowering and ripening of fruit. The seed is capable of growth from the beginning, but does not germinate until the spring comes. So it is with ideas. Every idea is abstractly possible at any period, but in the concrete cannot become a living growth either in the life of the individual or of society at any epoch indiscriminately. This would be possible only if thought were to be a mechanical process, the operation of an isolated reason. It is on the contrary a vital process of a living person, and therefore affected by the forces and states both of the individual and the community to which he belongs. An idea becomes powerful and fertile in a man only when its due season has come ; when his other ideas are so ordered that it can take its place among them ; when his soul gives it a vital response, and there are psychological tensions, which it relaxes or intensifies. And in society an idea becomes fruitful, takes root, and develops its intrinsic possibilities only when the soil is prepared for it.

Thus the idea—or rather the experience—of society has found its appointed hours. Only a little while ago man felt himself a self-contained microcosm. His ties with his fellow-men—the State for example, the family, affinity of ideas—he was apt to regard either as illusions or as institutions serving purely utilitarian ends or

92

assuring his safety. The one thing of which he was certain was himself, his existence in and for himself. Of others, and of fellowship with them, he was conscious only as something dubious and shadowy.

This was due to a psychological defect. He lacked the instinctive awareness of external reality, and in particular of other minds. He was not conscious of their inner life as a datum of his own experience, at least not as something actively affecting him. This attitude could find expression in totally different ways, from icy indifference to ruthless violence. A desire, it is true, for others made itself felt, the longing to be assured that a fellow-man is indeed there, a longing for understanding and comradeship. But it was always cut short by the despairing thought, 'It is impossible. I am imprisoned in my solitary isolation.' A fundamental sentiment of individualism cut men from their fellows.

If man was to escape despair or weary resignation, there remained nothing for him but to make a virtue of his dire necessity, and a very stern and bitter virtue it was. He must transform his yearning into pride, and his desire into refusal ; he must attempt to convince himself that 'the common life makes men common,' and a proud isolation is the only noble attitude.

But when men's eyes were opened, how false all this was seen to be ! They were opened, not by arguments— arguments are so weak in vital questions—but by a psychological transformation. Man became totally changed. New forces were at work in his soul, and he outgrew individualism. For his new outlook the possibility of a community has become self-evident. Nor does it arise from the deliberate conjunction of self-contained individuals. This is the erroneous conception which is impoverishing our social life and dividing the nations. No society is something to be taken for granted which requires no proof. It is as primary and as necessary as individuality. And to-day we ask ourselves how could we have put up so long with our self-imposed isolation.

Is not the present distress of Europe the last and most terrible spasm of this old disease ? When the right time comes, the perception will triumph that one nation is as dependent upon the others, as one individual upon his fellows. The doctrines of the philosophy of isolation have not succeeded in keeping men apart. They possessed a shadowy existence so long as men's souls were strangers to each other. But as soon as the social sense of community awoke, all such theories were swept away. For the nations also this spring will come. Their eyes will be opened ; and they will see that they belong to each other. On that day all doctrines of national selfishness, all the economic and political systems based on mistrust and mutual isolation, will vanish in smoke.

Yes, this experience of human community has come to many, and the rest have at least been influenced by it. The path to the souls of others lies open. What matter to us the doctrines of individualism, subjectivism, and solipsism ? Is the way to the soul of another man after all so much further than the path to my own ? The spell is dissolving. The common life does not make men common. That is true only of the wrong type of community. A good society is the source of happiness and power. It tests the pliability and power of resistance of our personality. It is in the highest sense a task, and a lofty enterprise.

*　　*　　*　　*　　*

So strong indeed has the will for community become—the word indeed, like every other valuable thing, is already deteriorating into a cheap slogan—that it is attracting men almost too powerfully to their fellows. Already we are becoming aware of the baneful possibilities of an exaggerated cult of the community. It is capable of destroying personality. We are beginning to understand the element of truth in the older individualism and to realise that society also has its problem.

The problem whether the souls of others are or are not accessible to us is not the only one. It was answered once and for all when man's fundamentally social nature was first experienced. But the answer has raised a further problem : what is the relation between the free individual and society ? What kind of society is valuable, what kind the reverse ? What kind of society is noble, what kind degrading ? Recognising independent personality and real community with others as the two poles of human life, we enquire, how should the one be constituted, if the other is to co-exist with it ? How is the one to be made perfect by the other ?

I will ask you to be patient while I tell you something about the last meeting of the Quickborn Association [1] at Burg Rothenfels. On that occasion the demands of the community were emphasised. The individual, we were told, is bound to his fellows by a natural loyalty, and is pledged to them with all he is and all he has. He must regard himself as a member of the same community with

[1] The Quickborn Association of Catholic Youth was founded in 1910, with Burg Rothenfels a. Main as its headquarters. Its aim is the permeation of the whole of life, literature, and art, with the Catholic spirit. In 1921 it numbered about 6,000 members. (Translator's Note.)

other classes and sections of his countrymen, giving to them all and receiving from them all.

Suddenly in the midst of these discussions, as though by a concerted plan, there sprang up at various points, and gathered strength, the idea of personality. The community must be so constituted that the dignity and inner freedom of the individual personality remain possible within it. For free personality is the presupposition of all true community. Those who grasped what was happening were astounded. Never before had I so profoundly experienced the power of life to maintain itself spontaneously, when it is not repressed by force.

This indeed is the supreme problem—how can a society be full-blooded and deep-rooted, a mutual surrender of its members' very selves, and at the same time inherited personality continue to flourish vigorously and freely?

Once more I must repeat, it is beyond the scope of man's natural powers. One of two things must happen. Either the power of community will burst all bounds, swamp the free personality of the individual, and strip him of spiritual dignity, or else the individual personality will assert itself victoriously, and in the process sever its organic bonds with the community. So deeply has original sin shattered the fundamental structure of human life.

But the Church stands before us as the one great Power which makes possible a perfect community when members are genuine personalities.

*   *   *   *   *

First and foremost she produces a true community. She effects a community of truth, the common possession those supreme supernatural realities of which faith makes us conscious. They are the foundations of the supernatural life, for all the same—God, Christ, grace, and the work of the Holy Spirit.

What does this mean for the community? All its members stand upon the same foundation. In all alike the same forces are at work. The same aims are acknowledged by all. Their judgments are based on the same standards of valuation. They recognise the same ideals of human moral perfection, and their fundamental dispositions are identical. In spite of all their dissimilarities, how close must be the bond between men, who take their Catholic faith seriously. How deep must be the knowledge one can have of another! For he knows the motives which finally decide his moral decisions and the beliefs which guide his conduct of life.

One man can have this knowledge of another because the lives of both are rooted in the same ultimate realities. One can help another, because he no longer need find reasons for trusting him. The deepest grounds of mutual trust are evident to both. Real consolation becomes possible, because its grounds are admitted by both parties. There is a common seriousness of purpose, a common consecration, and a common worship, for the same sublime facts and mysteries are honoured by all alike. There is a common endeavour and a common struggle, because the final aims of all are the same. There is a common joy —the joy of the Church's festivals—for a cause of rejoicing need not be sought far afield, and after anxious search. Joy is everywhere, and can therefore be a factor and bond of community.

There is also a community of sacrifice, a community of

mutual love, of command and obedience. No one can genuinely yield interior obedience if he is not aware of an ultimate bond between himself and his superior. But when he is aware of it, trust enters into his obedience, confidence into the command. Moreover, there can be no community of love without a bond, upon which the mutual self-surrender is based. Thus the community of truth becomes a community of love, of obedience, and of command. These, however, are the forces which constitute society, also the ways in which a bridge is built between man and man, by superiority, subordination, and equal co-operation.

And all this is realised, not timidly and distrustfully, but from a professed consciousness of interdependence, by a mutual trust, and responsibility. But this is possible only when that first fundamental community of truth exists, the foundation of all other manifestations of community.

*   *   *   *   *

There is a community of life, and it is immeasurably deep. The same current of grace flows through all alike, the same active power of God. The same real Christ is present in all, as the ideal and prime exemplar of perfection, our incentive to pursue it and the creative power which makes it possible.

The sacrament of community, Communion, is incomprehensible. In it man is one with God ; God is personally united with him, and is given to him as his very own. But with this one God not only one man is united, but all his fellows. And each receives God into his personal being ; yet each receives Him on behalf of the others also, on behalf of husband or wife, of children, parents, relatives, and friends—for all those to whom he is bound by ties of love.

There is a community of spirit and spiritual life—the mystical Body of Christ. Through Baptism the individual is born into it, into new, supernatural life common to all who live by it. But as yet he is merely a member of this organism. Confirmation makes him an adult member, and gives him rights, duties, and responsibilities in it. It gives him the commission and the power to pursue his calling as work for the Kingdom of God, with and for others. Holy Communion deepens his community with God, with others in God. By sin it is ruptured or impaired ; in the sacrament of Penance man acknowledges his fault before the divinely appointed representative of the ecclesiastical community, makes satisfaction to it, and is received back into it. Extreme Unction gives him the strength to remain loyal to it in sickness and death. Marriage intertwines the roots of the natural community of the individual and the race with those of the supernatural community. Finally, in Holy Orders, he who has been baptised and confirmed receives a power to act as God's representative, command and lead. Thus the sacraments are forms and processes, in which the life of the supernatural community begins, progresses, recovers lost ground, and is continually propagated.

Holy Mass is throughout a communal act. This truth has been widely forgotten. It has often been made the private devotion of the individual. But the evidence of the first Christian centuries proves its communal character to the hilt. The bishop officiated, and his priests concelebrated with him, as at the present day newly-consecrated priests concelebrate at their ordination. The people brought their gifts to the altar, and from among these were chosen the bread and the wine which were to be the material of the sacrifice offered for all. And these offerings were themselves recognised as symbols of the community. As the bread consists of many grains of wheat, and the wine has been pressed from a multitude of grapes, the mystical Body of Christ consists of many individuals. The people brought their offerings to the altar in person, that all might be drawn into the mystical unity to be effected when the substance of the bread and wine could be changed into the Body and Blood of Christ. All shared in the divine banquet, after they had banished from their hearts by the kiss of peace everything inimical to community life. When the sacred Bread was broken, portions were taken to prisoners and the sick. One bishop would send them to another, as a sign that all were united in a community transcending the limitations of space. And after each celebration a particle of the sacred Bread was preserved until the next and dipped in the Chalice, to show that this unity transcended time. To discover the roots of this sentiment we must read Our Lord's discourse after the Last Supper (John xiii–xvii.), and the Epistles of St. Paul and St. John. These sources bring home to us with an overwhelming force the fact that Christ instituted His Sacrifice and Sacrament as communal acts, expressions of the community between God and man, and between men in God, all ' in Christ,' Who ' has made us partakers of the divine nature.' Such was the belief and practice of the Apostles, and of the Church after them. Read what the Apostolic Fathers wrote on this topic, the epistles of St. Ignatius, for instance, and then above all read the liturgy itself. And though to-day, this com-

munal character of the liturgy is not clearly brought out
in its details, the Holy Sacrifice, or indeed the liturgy as a
whole, is intelligible only by those profoundly imbued
with the communal spirit and the will to participate in
the community life.

*　　*　　*　　*　　*

Contemplate for a moment those dogmas of the Church
specifically concerned with the Community.

In the beginning we find a community of responsibility
and destiny. So profound is the solidarity of mankind,
that the obedience of the first man would have been the
safeguard of all ; and his guilt was the guilt of all. This
is the mystery of original sin. It is intolerable to the
individualist, who has not grasped the extent of human
solidarity. But the man who has understood that every
self exists also in his neighbour ; that every man shares
the life of all other men, and that this happiness and
suffering are bound up with theirs, will realise that, in the
dogma of original sin, the Church has really touched the
very foundation of all human society.

But it is this very solidarity which makes the community of redemption possible. Since every man in his
profoundest being is thus bound up with his fellows, so
that another's guilt can become his, the atonement made
by the One can be the atonement made by all the rest.
God's Son becomes Man, and takes upon Himself the
guilt of the entire human race. This is no empty phrase,
or sublime imagination. Gethsemane is sufficient proof
that it was a most awful reality, a most real experience.
Jesus became our representative, and His sufferings thus
became the property of our race. He redeemed us, not

by His example, doctrine or instructions—all these are of secondary importance—but by the representative and atoning satisfaction in which He assumed before God the responsibility of our guilt. So far reaching is this objective community of atonement, that by its power any child, without any co-operation on its part, is reborn into a new life and mode of existence.

We now come to the solidarity between the regenerate, that is, the community or Communion of Saints. The one grace of Christ flows through them all as a single stream of life. All live by the same pattern, this example which influences them all. The one Holy Spirit is at work in them all. Each possesses grace not merely for himself, but for all the rest. He passes it on in every word, every encounter with others, every good thought, and every work of charity. Every increase of the grace he possesses, by the greater fidelity, the deepening and inner growth of his spiritual life which it effects, swells the stream of grace for all the others. Whenever an individual grows in knowledge and love, the others are also affected, and not only through speech, writing or visible example, but also directly, by an immediate and substantial transmission of love and light from soul to soul.

The prayer of my fellows, their works, their growth in grace and purity are mine also. When we encountered a pure and profound spirit—a man nearer to God than ourselves, and in whom the current of life flows fresh and strong—did we not form the wish, ' I would like a share in you ' ? In the Communion of Saints this actually comes to pass. There is something unutterably magnificent and profound in the thought that I am to share in all the purity and fulness of supernatural life hidden in the souls of others, and it is mine, too, in the solidarity of Christ's Body.

Have you ever thought about the community of suffering? Have you considered that one man transmits to another not only the force of example, speech and instruction, not only the superflux of grace and the efficacy of prayer and intercession, but also the power of suffering? Have you ever contemplated a truth of awe-inspiring profundity: that whenever one member offers his suffering to God for others in the community of Christ's Passion, that suffering becomes a life-giving and redeeming force for those for whom it has been offered up, and where nothing else could bring them help at any distance in space and in spite of any barriers intervening.

Not one of us knows to what extent he is living by the power of grace which flows into him through others—by the hidden prayer of the tranquil heart, the atoning sacrifices offered up by persons unknown to him, and the satisfaction made on his behalf by those who in silence offer themselves for their brethren. It is a community of the deepest and most intimate forces. They are silent, for nothing noisy can produce these substantial effects. But it cannot resist them because their source is God.

This community transcends all boundaries. It knows nothing of distance. It embraces all countries and peoples. It transcends the bounds of time, for in it the past is as active as the present. From this point, tradition, which is so often regarded in a purely external aspect, becomes a living realisation. And this community transcends the boundaries of this life, for it extends beyond the grave, embracing—both the Saints in Heaven, and the souls in Purgatory.

' That they all may be one ' : thus Christ prayed in the hour before His Passion : one in God, and one with each other. That prayer is being continually fulfilled in the Church.

The Church is ' the truth in love,' as St. Paul so magnificently describes it. She is truth, in the deepest sense of living truth, essential truth ; a flawless harmony of being, a divine fulness of life, a living creation. But it is a fulness of truth which is love, and is constantly striving to become a greater love. It is a light, which is at the same time a glowing heat, a treasure which cannot be contained in itself but must communicate itself to others, a stream which needs must flow, a possession which must be common to all, must give itself freely to all. The Church is love. She is truth, which communicates itself. She is the treasure, which must be the common property of all. She is the life, which multiplies itself, takes hold of all and of its very nature must be a common life, a life of boundless mutual donation in which all belongs to all.

*   *   *   *   *

Our contemplation must here ascend to the perfection and exemplar of society, the Triune God. My best utterance here is but a stammering. But permit me to speak as best I can.

God is the pure life of truth. Its fulness, however, is so vast that it is productive, and God possesses it as the Father—that is to say, as a generating Person—and transmits it to the Son. And when in turn—I speak according to our human usage, in terms of before and after, though in reality the whole process is eternal—the Son stands before the Father as the begotten Fulness of divine Truth, their mutual knowledge kindles a mutual and eternal love, and this love of Father and Son flames up as the Holy Ghost.

This community is infinite. It is an infinite life, an infinite possession, in which all things are mutually surrendered in perfect community. Everything is in common—life, power, truth, happiness—so perfectly indeed that there is no longer simply a possession of the same object, but the existence of identical life, and the community is an identity of the same substance and the same nature.

This divine community is externalised in the Church. For what is it that we then possess in common ? What is that All which we receive and give ? It is nothing less than the everlasting life of God, in which we are ' given a share ' through the mystery of regeneration, and which ever and again flows into us in the mystery of the Holy Communion. God is in me, and in you, and in us all. We are all born again from the Father, in Christ, through the Holy Ghost. He is in us, and we in Him. Only read those wonderful chapters of St. John which speak of this mystery, Our Lord's parting discourse to His disciples.

Yet all this is but feeble words. No human utterance can go further. At this point we may quote the final words of St. Bonaventure's treatise on the Ascent of the Spirit in God—(*Itinerarium Mentis in Deum*), when he tells his readers : ' If you desire further knowledge, question silence, not speech ; desire not the understanding ; the heartfelt utterance of prayer, not reading and study ; the bridegroom, not the teacher ; God, not men ; darkness, not daylight. Do not question light, but fire, the fire which kindles every heart it touches to a flame that rises up to God in the ecstasy of an overflowing heart and burning Love.'

This infinite mystery of truth which has become love, of a possession which belongs to all, this community without limit or end, this giving without reserve—that is the Church, the earthly extension of the divine community, the reflection of God's mutual self-donation. In his last work, which death did not allow him to finish, the ' Discourses on the Hexameron,' *Collationes in Hexameron*, St. Bonaventure has spoken most illuminatingly of this mystery. And you may gather further light from Scheeben's *Mysterien des Christentums* (Mysteries of the Christian Faith).

We have followed the mystery of society to its fountain-head—God. There, too, however, we find a counterpart to this society, namely, self-maintenance.

The Father bestows all things upon the Son, and Father and Son all things upon the Holy Ghost. All but one thing—the personal self. That remains immutably contained in itself. Personal unity, the dignity and sublimity of the self, can never be given away. In the process of mutual donation, in the excess of unity, we behold a point of rest, something abiding, surrounded by an impenetrable and sacred circle. It is personality. It can neither be given nor received. It rests in itself. In the very heart of the perfect society it stands alone, fixed in itself. This constitutes its essential inviolability. This inviolability of the person has its counterpart in God's relations with man. To be sure we all possess the same God. To every man He gives Himself and His entire self. But He gives Himself to each in a unique fashion, corresponding to his unique personality. In God we are all one, members of a community indescribably close. But at the same time each may be sure that God belongs to him in different fashion from that in which He belongs to anyone else, and that in this relationship, he is alone with God. The value of friendship is diminished when it is shared with many. But I know that God—and this is the miracle of His infinite life—belongs to all, but to each in a unique fashion. The holy circle of pure isolation surrounds that peace in which a man's inmost self is alone with his God.

And this law is repeated in every community worthy of the name. This is a truth of the first importance. A profound communal solidarity unites all the members of the Church, but in it the individual is never swallowed up in a featureless identity. It is often said that the communal life of the Church is cold. It is we who are cold, because we are still individualists. We all of us continue the frigid isolation of the social contract and the machine. But we desire to become wholly Catholic. Then, indeed, we shall experience the meaning of community. Then we shall become conscious of a living current passing from man to man, of the pulse throbbing from the heart of Christ through all His members. And yet that hallowed circle will always surround the inmost sanctuary and keep it inviolate. No one will be permitted to approach another too closely, to force his way into another man's soul, to lay a hand upon his inner independence, or override it. A profound reverence for human personality will govern everything. For it is the foundation of the Catholic style, whether solemn or joyful, in the Catholic manner of making requests or giving presents, the Catholic way of looking at things, the Catholic attitude : in short, of everything truly Catholic.[1]

[1] I should like here to sketch another line of thought. Catholicism regards every human being as the child of God. In this respect all are fundamentally equal. It is the human being alone that counts in all the essential religious relationships, such as in the Sacrifice of the Mass and in the Sacraments, in the approach to the various religious activities and responsibilities. I do not know if any other social organisation besides the Church exists, in which men meet so naturally as man to man, even if one of the parties is an officer of the society. In Confession, for instance, both priest and penitent are removed from their respective social positions, and confront each other in their essential characters. Within the spiritual sphere of the Church ' the soul,' ' the human being,' ' the priest,' ' the sinner,' ' the man,' ' the woman,' are in evidence, in short the entire collection of essential human types and aspects detached from their social environment. And this as a matter of course. Once the threshold of the Church is crossed, the fundamental categories of humanity occupy the scene. A simplification of the personality is effected. It is reduced to its essential human elements, cleared of all the obscurations introduced by human imperfections or the influences of a particular epoch. In this consists that unique sense of equality in the Church, which is the more perfect, because it passes without special notice.

On the other hand, the Church is the uncompromising foe of the ' democratic ' spirit, which would obliterate all distinctions of rank and natural capacity. In this sense she is whole-heartedly aristocratic. This is indeed involved in the tremendous power of tradition. ' Democratism ' —not democracy—is a wholly modern conception and a novelty. It makes genuine choice, valuation, and testing impossible. The power of tradition, on the contrary, compels the present to submit to a test and rejects those factors which are not strong enough to endure it. Kierkegaard's *Buch über Adler* has brought out in a very remarkable manner this selective and testing force of tradition. Authority also is aristocratic, if it really possesses the courage and strength to rule, and is not merely disguised weakness. The ' democratistic ' attitude of mind can neither command, nor obey.

Moreover, the Church, by her teaching and institutional embodiment of the evangelical counsels, has set before each one of us the possibility of an extraordinary vocation. She is charged with having established a double morality, one, more easy-going for the world, and another, more lofty code for the cloister. If old historical prejudices and scarcely disguised hatred did not stand in the way, it would soon be recognised that this economy is alone in accordance with man's nature. *From every man the Church requires perfection*—that is to say, with all his strength he must love God, do His Will, and work for His Kingdom in his particular sphere. She exhorts every man to grow more and more deeply into God,

Catholic commands are always inspired by reverence
for their subject. They are based upon the knowledge

and so by degrees to make his entire life the service of God, until he can
truly say, ' I live, now not I : but Christ liveth in me.'

This is the Christian attitude to life. It admits, however, an essential
difference in the rule of life which gives it practical embodiment. The
Christian attitude is the readiness to follow the path to which God is
calling. But He does not call all by the same road. The majority He calls
to follow the ordinary, a few the extraordinary road. The ordinary rule
of life is that in which the natural and supernatural values and demands
are brought into an harmonious balance. The extraordinary rule of life
is that in which even in the external conduct of life everything is directed
immediately to the supernatural. The former commanded ; the latter
counselled. The former is open to all men, the latter only to those ' who
can take it.' To deny that there is any difference between the two rules of
life is to deny the actual conditions of human existence. And it is untrue
to say that every man is suited to the extraordinary path. It is untrue
even in the natural sphere ; how much more therefore in the religious.
It is Philistinism and democratism which demand the abolition of the
extraordinary rule of life, that the follower of the ordinary path may not
suffer from a sense of inferiority. On the other hand it is fantastic—and
an extremely foolish and dangerous fantasy, too—to maintain that all are
called to follow the extraordinary path. Everyone who has once considered what this implies will agree. The Church distinguishes the two
rules. This expresses her aristocratic attitude, which refuses to surrender
to any cravings for equality.

Yet we can show that it is precisely by this distinction that each rule of
life makes the full development of the other possible, so that the complete
structure of human life can be built up. The rule of life in which the
extraordinary principle finds objective expression is that of the evangelical
counsels—poverty, chastity, and obedience. These are means by which
man in the concrete wholly transfers the momentum of his life to God,
places surrender at every point above self-preservation, the supernatural
above the natural. Actually the way of life resulting from these counsels
can either be followed freely ' in the world,' or else in the regulated forms
represented by religious orders. What, then, is the significance of the
latter for the community ? I am leaving out of account here the actual
services they perform, for example their care of the poor and the sick, the
intercession for the community made by the religious rule, who in their
contemplation present the entire human race to God. I am concerned
solely with the consideration of their sociological effect. The extraordinary fact of a perfect voluntary renunciation—and not as an ephemeral
exception, but as a perpetual phenomenon—gives that great majority
who follow the ordinary path, that independence of the possessions concerned, which is the more indispensable perquisite of their right use. To
take one instance ; marriage, is the isolation of two persons in God, and

that personality is sacred. To command in the Catholic style demands humility, not only from the man who

as a form of community, which is more than the mere sum of two partners and something higher, the image of God's Kingdom, the Church, and in every aspect as a fertility duly ordered. As such it cannot be established merely upon the basis of those natural forces which tend towards marriage. (To many this may seem a paradox; and it is. But when we have long pondered the forms of human life; the relation between their aims arising from their very nature and the forces actually at their disposal, the relation between one form and another; and the intrinsic economy of life, we come to understand that what superficially seems a paradox is often the only truly natural thing. Paradox is embedded in the very heart of normality. It is so here.) The forces which normally produce marriage are insufficient to make a marriage which fulfils its own inner nature. Such a marriage requires a perfect capacity of assent and surrender, but also an equally great independence of the sexual factor. Without the former the union is too superficial; without the latter it lacks inner dignity and the capacity for fidelity. Nature, however, cannot by itself produce this. It is only that perfect surrender in the conduct of life, which ' thinks only of the things that are God's,' which, by the constant influence it has exerted upon others through the centuries, awakens in the married also the strength requisite for complete surrender, with all the sacrifices that this entails. And their total renunciation of sex creates that freedom from the excessive power of sex, which in its turn reacts upon the mass of men and women and alone can make marriage faithful and chaste. To deny the possibility of this renunciation and surrender to God is also to deny man's noblest capacities and shake the foundation of true marriage. On the other hand, if a renunciation is to be truly heroic, the thing renounced must admittedly be valuable. An epoch must be fully aware of the value of marriage, of the treasures it comprises, if the sacrifice of the celibate is to be seen as something truly extraordinary. Marriage must display that profound inner wealth, must possess that nobility, must be that miraculous product fashioned by the co-operation of natural and supernatural forces, which Christ willed, Paul suggested, and the Church has always cherished. For the distinctive sacrifice in virginity is its renunciation of the perfect community and creative powers which only marriage can produce. Thus the loneliness of the extraordinary path can alone ensure that the rule, namely, marriage, shall become noble and profound. But conversely only marriage makes that sacrifice what it must be, if it is to realise the values inherent in its nature. Marriage, too, need be heroic, if the life of virginity is to escape the danger of becoming commonplace. The extraordinary is not heroic simply as such. On the contrary it consists in the perfect purity, generosity, and fidelity with which the extraordinary vocation is fulfilled. Similarly the ordinary is not of its nature commonplace. It also becomes heroic when it is realised with perfect purity, courage and fidelity. We must not confuse the obeys, but from the man who gives the command. It rejects violence, and the more completely, the more defenceless the subordinate in question. The Catholic superior knows that he is the servant of God's authority, and that it is his duty to increase by degrees the independence of his subordinates, and so make them as free as himself.

Catholic obedience is always dignified. It is not obsequious, or a weak leaning on the support of another, but the free and honourable submission to that reasonable obedience, in which the subject knows its limits, and keeps his own independence.

The Catholic way of sharing with others, of giving and receiving, is chaste. It never surrenders the final independence of the person, never breaks down that holy peace

characteristic distinctions between the two ways with distinctions of moral dispositions. There 'extraordinary' may also be very 'commonplace,' the ordinary very heroic. Marriage and virginity or more generally—the rule and the exception—duty and counsel—are forms of Christian life. 'Mediocre' and 'heroic,' on the contrary, are attitudes towards life. Every form of life can be lived in an heroic or in a mediocre spirit. And the resolve to live a life of heroic and unreserved self-devotion does not of itself determine the form of life in which it shall be accomplished. The 'good will' decides the former choice, 'vocation' the latter. We need men and women to live the extraordinary form of life heroically. But we have just as great need of others to live the ordinary form of life heroically. Heroism in marriage is just as indispensable as heroism in virginity. And it is certain that both types of heroism, viewed from the sociological standpoint, mutually support each other.

So deeply are aristocracy and—the right term does not exist—democracy interwoven in the Catholic spiritual order.

Those who take the right point of view will observe at every turn, with a delight mingled with a certain awe, how marvellously, how even uncannily right the Church is in all her values and arrangements; and how her attitude so commonly charged with hostility to life is in complete accord with life's most profound demands. We have, indeed, good cause to trust the Church! We have but to encounter such a masterpiece of the divine penetration and fashioning of human life, and all objections vanish into thin air. . . .

within which the soul enjoys her deepest community life, alone with God.

Catholic charity gives help, without wounding the recipient's dignity.

Catholic friendship recognises this mystery, and ensures that the parties to it always remain new to each other.

Catholic marriage is the perfect isolation of two human beings, and this is the source of its perennial youth.

All this is a sublime ideal. But it is the very soul of Catholic community life.

At Rothenfels one of those present remarked, ' Our fellowship must be such that its members are prepared if necessary to give and sacrifice all for each other. Nevertheless it does not proceed directly from man to man—that is the nature of fellowship in which free individuals bind themselves to their fellows by ties of friendship or love—but from me to God, and from God to you.' These words were spoken of a particular association. But they state a law which applies in some degree to every true community—however complete it may be, personality must remain inviolate. All community life presupposes this inner isolation.

And it is also the beginning and the end of form. For form signifies that there is a genuine community, but that it is limited in every direction by a consciousness of inner difference between man and man. Forms are but ways in which this fundamental attitude finds an appropriate expression in the various manifestations of community life, and becomes the law which preserves that life from corruption.

The road towards this goal, however, and not only for the élite alone, but for every man of good will, is the

Church. She makes it possible for ' all ' to ' be one,' and ' have all things common.' And she also brings home to us as a living conviction the fact that it does not profit a man ' if he gain the whole world and suffer the loss of his own soul.'

EPILOGUE

THESE lectures have not attempted to establish by scientific reasoning, but to state as my firm conviction, that the sphere of Catholic faith—the Church—is not merely one alternative among many, but religious truth, pure and simple, the Kingdom of God. The Church is not something belonging to the past, but absolute reality, and therefore the answer to every age, including our own, and its fulfilment. And this fulfilment will be the more perfect, the more substantial and the more complete our acceptance of the reality displayed by the Catholic faith and the more serious our endeavour to make our own the spiritual disposition it involves. This genuine Catholicity, which is seriously convinced of the supernatural and dogmatic character of Catholicism, is the most open-minded and the most comprehensive attitude, or rather the only open-minded comprehensive attitude, in existence. If by open-mindedness we mean the intellectual outlook which sees and values all objects as they really are, the Church can claim this description, because in face of the superabundant wealth of human experience she occupies the sole perfectly stable, clear and determined position. Both the wealth and the fixity enter into the Catholic mind. For the man whose outlook is narrow and timid, and whose experience of reality is impoverished, falls as far short of the Catholic outlook as the man who is incapable of an unconditional affirmative or negative, or who waters down her definitely supernatural teaching, or explains away the clear historical facts upon which it is based.

But more remains to be said. Already in my second lecture I pointed out that we are concerned with the actual, not the ideal Church, not with a spiritual one, but the historical Church as she exists to-day. The Church is not an ideal, which can be constructed *à priori*, and upon which we may fall back when reality fails us, as, for instance, we may elaborate an ideal state. Fundamentally there is no such thing as a philosophy of the Church. She is on the contrary a unique fact. Her position in this respect resembles that of a man. If anyone were to say that a particular judgment was applicable not to his friend in the concrete, but only to his ideal, and in consequence were to divert his approval from the man to the ideal, he would be guilty of an injustice to his friend's personality. It would indeed be worse than an injustice ; it would be disloyalty. For it would be a complete blindness to the essential decision with which human personality confronts us to accept or refuse it as it actually is. It demands yes or no, hostility or loyalty, but cannot admit a retreat into the abstract and a denial of reality in the name of the ideal. Such an attribute would be metaphysically false, because it would ignore the essential nature of individual personality by treating it as nothing more than a particular instance of a universal, and it would be morally unacceptable, because it would substitute for the attitude which must be adopted towards a person the attitude proper in the case of a mere thing. It is equally irrational to distinguish between the reality and the ideal of the Church. This, however, makes a further distinction the more indispensable. We must enquire whether the real inner form of the Church, her inner perfection ordained by God, is revealed by any given external of manifestation. Are forces which spring from her very essence fully operative in the visible expressions of her life ? Is her inner nature visible in her members ? No one can evade this question, for it concerns each one of us personally. When a man reaches the conviction that the Church is absolute in her actual nature and in every age teaches the way to perfection and the strength by which it may be achieved, his immediate reaction will be an intense gratitude. But this gratitude must not induce him to settle down in spiritual comfort, but must be felt as a demand. The parable of the talents is applicable also to our relation to the Church. We are all responsible for her, each in his own way, the priest in virtue of his Ordination, the layman in virtue of his Confirmation. Upon each one of us depends the degree of harmony achieved between the nature of the Church and her outward semblance, between her inner and outer aspects. Here, too, we bear a heavy responsibility towards those outside the Church. It requires the vision of love and of faith to see the inner nature of the Church beneath expressions often so defective. Even her own members sometimes lack this vision. How much less then is it to be expected from those who regard the Church with distrust as strangers, blinded by the prejudices and false values of their education ! We cannot blame them if they regard the assertions made in these lectures as theorising. For it is indeed true that a valid argument in this sphere should be conducted by Catholics, whose lives inspire confidence. Their proofs, it is true, are not without their intrinsic value. But their power to bring conviction is strongest when they are supported by a living ' proof of power.'

THE SPIRIT OF THE LITURGY

THE
SPIRIT OF THE LITURGY

I

THE PRAYER OF THE LITURGY

An old theological proverb says, 'Nothing done by nature and grace is done in vain.' Nature and grace obey their own laws, which are based upon certain established hypotheses. Both the natural and the supernatural life of the soul, when lived in accordance with these principles, remain healthy, develop, and are enriched. In isolated cases the rules may be waived without any danger, when such a course is required or excused by reason of a spiritual disturbance, imperative necessity, extraordinary occasion, important end in view, or the like. In the end, however, this cannot be done with impunity. Just as the life of the body droops and is stunted when the conditions of its growth are not observed, so it is with spiritual and religious life—it sickens, losing its vigour, strength and unity.

This is even more true where the regular spiritual life of a corporate body is concerned. Exceptions play a far greater part, after all, in the life of the individual than in that of the group. As soon as a group is in question, concern is immediately aroused with regard to the regulation of those practices and prayers which will constitute the permanent form of its devotion in common ; and then the crucial question arises whether the fundamental laws which govern normal interior life—in the natural as in the supernatural order—are in this case to have currency or not. For it is no longer a question of the correct attitude to be adopted, from the spiritual point of view, towards the adjustment of some temporary requirement or need, but of the form to be taken by the permanent legislation which will henceforth exercise an enduring influence upon the soul. This is not intended to regulate entirely independent cases, each on its own merits, but to take into account the average requirements and demands of everyday life. It is not to serve as a model for the spiritual life of the individual, but for that of a corporate body, composed of the most distinct and varied elements. From this it follows that any defect in its organisation will inevitably become both apparent and obtrusive. It is true that at first every mistake will be completely overshadowed by the particular circumstances—the emergency or disturbance—which justified the adoption of that particular line of conduct. But in proportion as the extraordinary symptoms subside, and the normal existence of the soul is resumed, the more forcibly every interior mistake is bound to come to light, sowing destruction on all sides in its course.

The fundamental conditions essential to the full expansion of spiritual life as it is lived in common are most clearly discernible in the devotional life of any great community which has spread its development over a long period of time. Its scheme of life has by then matured and developed its full value. In a corporate body—composed of people of highly varied circumstances, drawn from distinct social strata, perhaps even from different races, in the course of different historical and cultural periods—the ephemeral, adventitious, and locally characteristic elements are, to a certain extent, eliminated, and that which is universally accepted as binding and essential comes to the fore. In other words, the canon of spiritual administration becomes, in the course of time, objective and impartial.

The Catholic liturgy is the supreme example of an objectively established rule of spiritual life. It has been able to develop κατὰ τὸν ὅλον, that is to say, in every direction, and in accordance with all places, times, and types of human culture. Therefore it will be the best teacher of the *via ordinaria*—the regulation of religious life in common, with, at the same time, a view to actual needs and requirements.[1]

The significance of the liturgy must, however, be more exactly defined. Our first task will be to establish the quality of its relation to the non-liturgical forms of spiritual life.

The primary and exclusive aim of the liturgy is not the expression of the individual's reverence and worship for God. It is not even concerned with the awakening, formation, and sanctification of the individual soul as such. Nor does the onus of liturgical action and prayer rest with the individual. It does not even rest with the collective groups, composed of numerous individuals, who periodic-

[1] It is not by chance that ' the religious Pope ' so resolutely took in hand the revision of the liturgy. The internal revival of the Catholic community will not make progress until the liturgy again occupies its rightful position in Catholic life. And the Eucharistic movement can only effectually distribute its blessings when it is in close touch with the liturgy. It was the Pope who issued the Communion Decrees who also said, ' You must not *pray* at Mass, you must *say* Mass ! ' Only when the Blessed Sacrament is understood from the point of view of the liturgy can It take that active share in the religious regeneration of the world which Pius X expected of It. (In the same way the full active and moral power of the Blessed Sacrament is only free to operate unchecked when Its connection with the problems and tasks of public and family life, and with those of Christian charity and of vocational occupations, is fully comprehended.)

ally achieve a limited and intermittent unity in their capacity as the congregation of a church. The liturgical entity consists rather of the united body of the faithful as such—the Church—a body which infinitely outnumbers the mere congregation. The liturgy is the Church's public and lawful act of worship, and it is performed and conducted by the officials whom the Church herself has designated for the post—her priests. In the liturgy God is to be honoured by the body of the faithful, and the latter is in its turn to derive sanctification from this act of worship. It is important that this objective nature of the liturgy should be fully understood. Here the Catholic conception of worship in common sharply differs from the Protestant, which is predominatingly individualistic. The fact that the individual Catholic, by his absorption into the higher unity, finds liberty and discipline, originates in the twofold nature of man, who is both social and solitary.

Now, side by side with the strictly ritual and entirely objective forms of devotion, others exist, in which the personal element is more strongly marked. To this type belong those which are known as ' popular devotions,' such as afternoon prayers accompanied by hymns, devotions suited to varying periods, localities, or requirements, and so on. They bear the stamp of their time and surroundings, and are the direct expression of the characteristic quality or temper of an individual congregation.

Although in comparison with the prayer of the individual, which is expressive of purely personal needs and aspirations, popular devotions are both communal and objective, they are to a far greater degree characteristic of their origin than is the liturgy, the entirely objective and impersonal method of prayer practised by the Church as a whole. This is the reason for the greater stress laid by popular devotion upon the individual need of edification. Hence the rules and forms of liturgical practice cannot be taken, without more ado, as the authoritative and decisive standard for non-liturgical prayer. The claim that the liturgy should be taken as the exclusive pattern of devotional practice in common can never be upheld. To do so would be to confess complete ignorance of the spiritual requirements of the greater part of the faithful. The forms of popular piety should rather continue to exist side by side with those of the liturgy, and should constitute themselves according to the varying requirements of historical, social, and local conditions. There could be no greater mistake than that of discarding the valuable elements in the spiritual life of the people for the sake of the liturgy, or than the desire of assimilating them to it. But in spite of the fact that the liturgy and popular devotion have each their own special premises and aims, still it is to liturgical worship that pre-eminence of right belongs. The liturgy is and will be the *lex orandi*. Non-liturgical prayer must take the liturgy for its model, and must renew itself in the liturgy, if it is to retain its vitality. It cannot precisely be said that as dogma is to private religious opinion, so is the liturgy to popular devotion; but the connection between the latter does to a certain degree correspond with that special relation, characteristic of the former, which exists between the government and the governed. All other forms of devotional practice can always measure their shortcomings by the standard of the liturgy, and with its help find the surest way back to the *via ordinaria* when they have strayed from it. The changing demands of time, place, and special circumstance can express themselves in popular devotion ; facing the latter stands the liturgy, from which clearly issue the fundamental laws—eternally and universally unchanging —which govern all genuine and healthy piety.

In the following pages an attempt will be made to select from the liturgy and to analyse several of these laws. But it is an attempt pure and simple, which professes to be neither exhaustive nor conclusive.

The first and most important lesson which the liturgy has to teach is that the prayer of a corporate body must be sustained by thought. The prayers of the liturgy are entirely governed by and interwoven with dogma. Those who are unfamiliar with liturgical prayer often regard them as theological formulæ, artistic and didactic, until on closer acquaintance they suddenly perceive and admit that the clear-cut, lucidly constructed phrases are full of interior enlightenment. To give an outstanding example, the wonderful Collects of the Masses of Sunday may be quoted. Wherever the stream of prayer wells abundantly upwards, it is always guided into safe channels by means of plain and lucid thought. Interspersed among the pages of the Missal and the Breviary are readings from Holy Scripture and from the works of the Fathers, which continually stimulate thought. Often these readings are introduced and concluded by short prayers of a characteristically contemplative and reflective nature—the antiphons —during which that which has been heard or read has time to cease echoing and to sink into the mind. The liturgy, the *lex orandi*, is, according to the old proverb, the law of faith—the *lex credendi*—as well. It is the treasure-house of the thought of Revelation.

This is not, of course, an attempt to deny that the heart and the emotions play an important part in the life of prayer. Prayer is, without a doubt, 'a raising of the heart to God.' But the heart must be guided, supported, and purified by the mind. In individual cases or on definite and explicit occasions it may be possible to persist in, and to derive benefit from, emotion pure and simple, either spontaneous or occasioned by a fortunate chance. But a regular and recurrent form of devotion lights upon the most varied moods, because no one day resembles another. If the content of these devotional forms is of a predominatingly emotional character, it will bear the stamp of its fortuitous origin, since the feeling engendered by solitary spiritual occurrences flows for the most part into special and particular channels. Such a prayer therefore will always be unsuitable if it does not harmonise, to a certain degree at least, with the disposition of the person who is to offer it. Unless this condition is complied with, either it is useless or it may even mar the sentiment experienced. The same thing occurs when a form of prayer intended for a particular purpose is considered to be adapted to the most varied occasions.

Only thought is universally current and consistent, and, as long as it is really thought, remains suited, to a certain degree, to every intelligence. If prayer in common, therefore, is to prove beneficial to the majority, it must be primarily directed by thought, and not by feeling. It is only when prayer is sustained by and steeped in clear and fruitful religious thought, that it can be of service to a corporate body, composed of distinct elements, all actuated by varying emotions.

We have seen that thought alone can keep spiritual life

sound and healthy. In the same way, prayer is beneficial only when it rests on the bedrock of truth. This is not meant in the purely negative sense that it must be free from error; in addition to this, it must spring from the fulness of truth. It is only truth—or dogma, to give it its other name—which can make prayer efficacious, and impregnate it with that austere, protective strength without which it degenerates into weakness. If this is true of private prayer, it is doubly so of popular devotion, which in many directions verges on sentimentality.[1] Dogmatic thought brings release from the thraldom of individual caprice, and from the uncertainty and sluggishness which follow in the wake of emotion. It makes prayer intelligible, and causes it to rank as a potent factor in life.

If, however, religious thought is to do justice to its mission, it must introduce into prayer truth in all its fulness.

Various individual truths of Revelation hold a special attraction for the temperaments and conditions to which they correspond. It is easy to see that certain people have a pronounced predilection for certain mysteries of faith. This is shown in the case of converts, for instance, by the religious ideas which first arrested their attention at their entry into the Church, or which decided them on the step they were taking, and in other cases by the truths which at the approach of doubt form the mainstay and buttress of the whole house of faith. In the same way doubt does not charge at random, but attacks for the most part those

---

[1] A proof of this is to be found in the often sugary productions of sacred art—holy pictures, statues, etc.—which appeal to the people. The people are susceptible to powerful art when it is national; the Middle Ages are a witness to this, and certain aspects of modern art. But the danger of lapsing into mere insipidity is very great. The same thing applies to popular songs, and holds good in other directions as well.

mysteries of faith which appeal least to the temperament of the people concerned.[1]

If a prayer therefore stresses any one mystery of faith in an exclusive or an excessive manner, in the end it will adequately satisfy none but those who are of a corresponding temperament, and even the latter will eventually become conscious of their need of truth in its entirety. For instance, if a prayer deals exclusively with God's mercy, it will not ultimately satisfy even a delicate and tender piety, because this truth calls for its complement— the fact of God's justice and majesty. In any form of prayer, therefore, which is intended for the ultimate use of a corporate body, the whole fulness of religious truth must be included.

Here, too, the liturgy is our teacher. It condenses into prayer the entire body of religious truth. Indeed, it is nothing else but truth expressed in terms of prayer. For it is the great fundamental truths [2] which above all fill the liturgy—God in His mighty reality, perfection, and greatness, One, and Three in One ; His creation, providence, and omnipresence ; sin, justification, and the desire of salvation ; the Redeemer and His kingdom ; the four last things. It is only such an overwhelming abundance of truth which can never pall, but continue to be, day after day, all things to all men, ever fresh and inexhaustible.

[1] This does not mean that these truths are merely a mental indication of the existing spiritual condition of the person concerned. It is rather a proof of the saying, ' grace takes nature for granted.' Revelation finds in a man's natural turn of mind the necessary spiritual premises by which the truths, which are of themselves mysteries, can be more easily grasped and adhered to.

[2] It is a further proof of Pius X's perspicacity that he made universally accessible precisely those portions of the liturgy—Sundays, the weekly office, and especially the daily Masses of Lent—which stress the great fundamental mysteries of faith.

In the end, therefore, prayer in common will be fruitful only in so far as it does not concentrate markedly, or at any rate exclusively, on particular portions of revealed truth, but embraces, as far as possible, the whole of Divine teaching. This is especially important where the people are concerned, because they easily tend to develop a partiality for particular mysteries of faith which for some reason have become dear to them.[1] On the other hand, it is obvious that prayer must not be overladen and as a result form a mere hotchpotch of ill-assorted thoughts and ideas—a thing which sometimes does occur. Yet without the element of spaciousness, spiritual life droops and becomes narrow and petty. ' The truth shall make you free '—free not only from the thraldom of error, but free as a preparation for the vastness of God's kingdom.

While the necessity of thought is emphasised, it must not be allowed to degenerate into the mere frigid domination of reason. Devotional forms on the contrary should be permeated by warmth of feeling.

On this point as well the liturgy has many recommendations to make. The ideas which fill it are vital : that is to say, they spring from the impulses of the heart which has been moulded by grace, and must again in their turn affect other eager and ardent hearts. The Church's worship is full of deep feeling, of emotion that is intense, and sometimes even vehement. Take the Psalms, for instance—how deeply moving they often are ! Listen to the expression of longing in the *Quemadmodum*, of remorse

---

[1] By this we do not mean that specific times (*e.g.*, the stress of war) and conditions (*e.g.*, the special needs of an agricultural or seafaring population) do not bring home certain truths more vividly than others. We are dealing here with the universal principle, which is, however, adaptable and must make allowances for special cases.

in the *Miserere*, of exultation in the Psalms of praise, and of indignant righteousness in those denouncing the wicked. Or consider the remarkable spiritual tension which lies between the mourning of Good Friday and the joy of Easter morning.

Liturgical emotion is, however, exceedingly instructive. It has its moments of supreme climax, in which all bounds are broken, as, for instance, in the limitless rejoicing of the *Exultet* on Holy Saturday. But as a rule it is controlled and subdued. The heart speaks powerfully, but thought at once takes the lead ; the forms of prayer are elaborately constructed, the constituent parts carefully counterbalanced ; and as a rule they deliberately keep emotion under strict control. In this way, in spite of the deep feeling to be found in, say, the Psalms (to instance them once more), a sense of restraint pervades liturgical form.

The liturgy as a whole is not favourable to exuberance of feeling. Emotion glows in its depths, but it smoulders merely, like the fiery heart of the volcano, whose summit stands out clear and serene against the quiet sky. The liturgy *is* emotion, but it is emotion under the strictest control. We are made particularly aware of this at Holy Mass, and it applies equally to the prayers of the Ordinary and of the Canon, and to those of the Proper of the Time. Among them are to be found masterpieces of spiritual restraint.

The restraint characteristic of the liturgy is at times very pronounced—so much so as to make this form of prayer appear at first as a frigid intellectual production, until we gradually grow familiar with it and realise what vitality pulsates in the clear, measured forms.

And how necessary this discipline is ! At certain moments and on certain occasions it is permissible for emotion to have a vent. But a prayer which is intended for the everyday use of a large body of people must be restrained. If, therefore, it has uncontrolled and unbalanced emotion for a foundation, it is doubly dangerous. It will operate in one of two ways. Either the people who use it will take it seriously, and probably will then feel obliged to force themselves into acquiescence with an emotion that they have never, generally speaking, experienced, or which, at any rate, they are not experiencing at that particular moment, thus perverting and degrading their religious feeling. Or else indifference, if they are of a phlegmatic temperament, will come to their aid ; they then take the phrases at less than their face value, and consequently the word is depreciated.

Written prayer is certainly intended as a means of instruction and of promoting an increased sensibility. But its remoteness from the average emotional attitude must not be allowed to become too great. If prayer is ultimately to be fruitful and beneficial to a corporate body, it must be intense and profound, but at the same time normally tranquil in tone. The wonderful verses of the hymn—hardly translatable, so full are they of penetrating insight—may be quoted in this connection :

> *Laeti bibamus sobriam*
> *Ebrietatem Spiritus . . .*[1]

Certainly we must not try to measure off the lawful share

[1] From the Benedictine Breviary, Lauds (*i.e.*, the prayer at daybreak) of Tuesday. [Literally, ' Let us joyfully taste of the sober drunkenness of the Spirit.']

of emotion with a foot-rule; but where a plain and straightforward expression suffices we must not aggrandise nor embellish it; and a simple method of speech is always to be preferred to an overloaded one.

Again, the liturgy has many suggestions to make on the quality of the emotion required for the particular form of prayer under discussion, which is ultimately to prove universally beneficial. It must not be too choice in expression, nor spring from special sections of dogma, but clearly express the great fundamental feelings, both natural and spiritual, as do the Psalms, for instance, where we find the utterance of adoration, longing for God, gratitude, supplication, awe, remorse, love, readiness for sacrifice, courage in suffering, faith, confidence, and so on. The emotion must not be too acutely penetrating, too tender, or too delicate, but strong, clear, simple and natural.

Then the liturgy is wonderfully reserved. It scarcely expresses, even, certain aspects of spiritual surrender and submission, or else it veils them in such rich imagery that the soul still feels that it is hidden and secure. The prayer of the Church does not probe and lay bare the heart's secrets; it is as restrained in thought as in imagery; it does, it is true, awaken very profound and very tender emotions and impulses, but it leaves them hidden. There are certain feelings of surrender, certain aspects of interior candour which cannot be publicly proclaimed, at any rate in their entirety, without danger to spiritual modesty. The liturgy has perfected a masterly instrument which has made it possible for us to express our inner life in all its fulness and depth, without divulging our secrets—*secretum meum mihi*. We can pour out our hearts, and still feel that nothing has been dragged to light that should remain hidden.[1]

This is equally true of the system of moral conduct which is to be found in prayer.

Liturgical action and liturgical prayer are the logical consequences of certain moral premises—the desire for justification, contrition, readiness for sacrifice, and so on —and often issue afresh into moral actions. But there again it is possible to observe a fine distinction. The liturgy does not lightly exact moral actions of a very far-reaching nature, especially those which denote an interior decision. It requires them where the matter is of real importance, *e.g.*, the abjuration at baptism, or the vows at the final reception into an order. When, however, it is a question of making regular daily prayer fruitful in every-day intentions and decisions, the liturgy is very cautious. For instance, it does not rashly utter such things as vows, or full and permanent repudiations of sin, entire and lasting surrender, all-embracing consecration of one's entire being, utter contempt for and renouncement of the world, promises of exclusive love, and the like. Such ideas are present at times, fairly frequently even, but generally under the form of a humble entreaty that the suppliant

[1] The liturgy here accomplishes on the spiritual plane what has been done on the temporal by the dignified forms of social intercourse, the outcome of the tradition created and handed down by sensitive people. This makes communal life possible for the individual, and yet insures him against unauthorised interference with his inner self; he can be cordial without sacrificing his spiritual independence; he is in communication with his neighbour without on that account being swallowed up and lost among the crowd. In the same way the liturgy preserves freedom of spiritual movement for the soul by means of a wonderful union of spontaneity and the finest erudition. It extols *urbanitas* as the best antidote to barbarism, which triumphs when spontaneity and culture alike are no more.

may be vouchsafed similar sentiments, or that he is encouraged to ponder upon their goodness and nobility, or is exhorted on the same subject. But the liturgy avoids the frequent use of those prayers in which these moral actions are specifically expressed.

How right this is ! In moments of exaltation and in the hour of decision such a manner of speech may be justified, and even necessary. But when it is a question of the daily spiritual life of a corporate body, such formulas, when frequently repeated, offer those who are using them an unfortunate selection from which to make their choice. Perhaps they take the formulas literally and endeavour to kindle the moral sentiments expressed in them, discovering later that it is often difficult, and sometimes impossible, to do so truthfully and effectually. They are consequently in danger of developing artificial sentiments, of forcing intentions that still remain beyond their compass, and of daily performing moral actions, which of their very nature cannot be frequently accomplished. Or else they take the words merely as a passing recommendation of a line of conduct which it would be well to adopt, and in this way depreciate the intrinsic moral value of the formula, although it may be used frequently, and in all good faith. In this connection are applicable the words of Christ, ' Let your speech be yea, yea,—nay, nay.' [1]

The liturgy has solved the problem of providing a constant incentive to the highest moral aims, and at the same time of remaining true and lofty, while satisfying everyday needs.

Another question which arises is that concerning the form to be taken by prayer in common. We may put it

[1] Matt. v. 37.

like this : What method of prayer is capable of transforming the souls of a great multitude of people, and of
making this transformation permanent ?

The model of all devotional practice in common is to
be found in the Divine Office, which day after day gathers
together great bodies of people at stated times for a particular purpose. If anywhere, then it is in the Office that
those conditions will be found which are favourable to
the framing of rules for the forms of prayer in common.[1]

It is of paramount importance that the whole gathering
should take an active share in the proceedings. If those
composing the gathering merely listen, while one of the
number acts as spokesman, the interior movement soon
stagnates. All present, therefore, are obliged to take part.
It is not even sufficient for the gathering to do so by
repeating the words of their leader. This type of prayer
does, of course, find a place in the liturgy, *e.g.*, in the
litany. It is perfectly legitimate, and people desirous of
abandoning it totally fail to recognise the requirements of
the human soul. In the litany the congregation answers
the varying invocations of the leader with an identical act,
e.g., with a request. In this way the act each time acquires
a fresh content and fresh fervour, and an intensification of
ardour is the result. It is a method better suited than any
other to express a strong, urgent desire, or a surrender to
God's Will, presenting as it does the petition of all sides
effectively and simultaneously.

But the liturgy does not employ this method of prayer

[1] We do not overlook the fact that the Office in its turn presupposes
its special relations and conditions, from which useful hints may be gained
for private devotion, such as the necessity for a great deal of leisure, which
enables the soul to meditate more deeply ; and a special erudition, which
opens the mind to the world of ideas and to artistry of form, and so on.

frequently; we may even say, when we consider divine worship as a whole, that it employs it but seldom. And rightly so, for it is a method which runs the risk of numbing and paralysing spiritual movement.[1] The liturgy adapts the dramatic form by choice to the fundamental requirements of prayer in common. It divides those present into two choirs, and causes prayer to progress by means of dialogue. In this way all present join the proceedings, and are obliged to follow with a certain amount of attention at least, knowing as they do that the continuation of their combined action depends upon each one personally.

Here the liturgy lays down one of the fundamental principles of prayer, which cannot be neglected with impunity.[2] However justified the purely responsive forms of prayer may be, the primary form of prayer in common is the actively progressive—that much we learn from the *lex orandi*. And the question, intensely important to-day,

[1] The foregoing remarks on the liturgy have already made it abundantly clear that the justification of methods of prayer such as, *e.g.*, the Rosary, must not be gainsaid. They have a necessary and peculiar effect in the spiritual life. They clearly express the difference which exists between liturgical and popular prayer. The liturgy has for its fundamental principle, *Ne bis idem* [there must be no repetition]. It aims at a continuous progress of ideas, mood and intention. Popular devotion, on the contrary, has a strongly contemplative character, and loves to linger around a few simple images, ideas and moods without any swift changes of thought. For the people the forms of devotion are often merely a means of being with God. On this account they love repetition. The ever-renewed requests of the Our Father, Hail Mary, etc., are for them at the same time receptacles into which they can pour their hearts.

[2] In earlier ages the Church practised by preference the so-called ' responsive ' form of chanting the Psalms. The Precentor chanted one verse after the other, and the people answered with the identical verse, or the partially repeated verse. But at the same time another method was in use, according to which the people divided into two choirs, and each alternately chanted a verse of the Psalm. It says much for the sureness of liturgical instinct that the second method entirely supplanted the first. (Cf. Thalhofer-Eisenhofer, *Handbuch der katholischen Liturgik*, Freiburg, 1902, I, 261 *et seq.*)

as to the right method to employ in again winning people to the life of the Church is most closely connected with the question under discussion. For it is modern people precisely who insist upon vital and progressive movement, and an active share in things. The fluid mass of this overwhelming spiritual material, however, needs cutting down and fashioning. It requires a leader to regulate the beginning, omissions, and end, and, in addition, to organise the external procedure. The leader also has to model it interiorly ; thus, for instance, he has to introduce the recurrent thought-theme, himself undertaking the harder portions, in order that they may be adequately and conscientiously dealt with ; he must express the emotion of all present by means of climaxes, and introduce certain restful pauses by the inclusion of didactic or meditative portions. Such is the task of the choir-leader, which has undergone a carefully graduated course of development in the liturgy.

Attention has already been called to the deep and fruitful emotion which is contained in the liturgy. It also embraces the two fundamental forces of human existence : Nature and civilisation.

In the liturgy the voice of Nature makes itself heard clearly and decisively. We only need to read the Psalms to see man as he really is. There the soul is shown as courageous and despondent, happy and sorrowful, full of noble intentions, but of sin and struggles as well, zealous for everything that is good and then again apathetic and dejected. Or let us take the readings from the Old Testament. How frankly human nature is revealed in them ! There is no attempt at extenuation or excuse. The same thing applies to the Church's words of ordination, and to the prayers used in administering the sacraments. A truly refreshing spontaneity characterises them ; they call things by their names. Man is full of weakness and error, and the liturgy acknowledges this. Human nature is inexplicable, a tangled web of splendour and misery, of greatness and baseness, and as such it appears in the prayer of the Church. Here we find no carefully adapted portrait from which the harsh and unpleasing traits have been excluded, but man as he is.

Not less rich is the liturgy's cultural heritage. We become conscious of the fact that many centuries have co-operated in its formation and have bequeathed to it of their best. They have fashioned its language ; expanded its ideas and conceptions in every direction ; developed its beauty of construction down to the smallest detail—the short verses and the finely-forged links of the prayers, the artistic form of the Divine Office and of the Mass, and the wonderful whole that is the ecclesiastical year. Action, narrative, and choral forms combine to produce the cumulative effect. The style of the individual forms continually varies—simple and clear in the Hours, rich in mystery on the festivals of Mary, resplendent on the more modern feasts, delightful and full of charm in the offices of the early virgin-martyrs. To this we should add the entire group of ritual gestures and action, the liturgical vessels and vestments, and the works of sculptors and artists and musicians.

In all this is to be learnt a really important lesson on liturgical practice. Religion needs civilisation. By civilisation we mean the essence of the most valuable products of man's creative, constructive, and organising powers— works of art, science, social orders, and the like. In the liturgy it is civilisation's task to give durable form and expression to the treasure of truths, aims, and supernatural activity, which God has delivered to man by Revelation, to distil its quintessence, and to relate this to life in all its multiplicity. Civilisation is incapable of creating a religion, but it can supply the latter with a *modus operandi*, so that it can freely engage in its beneficent activity. That is the real meaning of the old proverb, *Philosophia ancilla theologiæ*—philosophy is the handmaid of theology. It applies to all the products of civilisation, and the Church has always acted in accordance with it. Thus she knew very well what she was doing, for instance, when she absolutely obliged the Order of Saint Francis—brimming over with high aspirations, and spiritual energy and initiative—to adopt a certain standard of living, property, learning, and so on. Only a prejudiced mind, with no conception of the fundamental conditions essential to normal spiritual life, would see in this any deterioration of the first high aims. By her action in the matter the Church, on the contrary, prepared the ground for the Order, so that in the end it could remain healthy and productive. Individuals, or short waves of enthusiasm, can to a wide degree dispense with learning and culture. This is proved by the beginnings of the desert Orders in Egypt, and of the mendicant friars, and by holy people in all ages. But, generally speaking, a fairly high degree of genuine learning and culture is necessary in the long run, in order to keep spiritual life healthy. By means of these two things spiritual life retains its energy, clearness, and catholicity. Culture preserves spiritual life from the unhealthy, eccentric, and one-sided elements with which it tends to get involved only too easily. Culture enables religion to express itself, and helps it to distinguish what is essential from what is non-essential, the means from the end, and the path from the goal. The Church has always condemned every attempt at attacking science, art, property, and so on. The same Church which so resolutely stresses the 'one thing necessary,' and which upholds with the greatest impressiveness the teaching of the Evangelical Counsels—that we must be ready to sacrifice everything for the sake of eternal salvation—nevertheless desires, as a rule, that spiritual life should be impregnated with the wholesome salt of genuine and lofty culture.

But spiritual life is in precisely as great a need of the subsoil of healthy nature—' grace takes nature for granted.' The Church has clearly shown her views on the subject by the gigantic struggles waged against Gnosticism and Manicheeism, against the Catharists and the Albigenses, against Jansenism and every kind of fanaticism. This was done by the same Church which, in the face of Pelagius and Celestius, of Jovinian and Helvidius, and of the immoderate exaltation of nature, powerfully affirmed the existence of grace and of the supernatural order, and asserted that the Christian must overcome nature. The lack of fruitful and lofty culture causes spiritual life to grow numbed and narrow ; the lack of the subsoil of healthy nature makes it develop on mawkish, perverted, and unfruitful lines. If the cultural element of prayer declines, the ideas become impoverished, the language coarse, the imagery clumsy and monotonous ; in the same way, when the life-blood of nature no longer flows vigorously in its veins, the ideas become empty and tedious, the emotion paltry and artificial, and the imagery lifeless and inspid. Both—the lack of natural vigour and the lack of lofty culture—together constitute what we call barbarism, *i.e.*, the exact contradiction of that ' *scientia vocis* ' which is revealed in liturgical prayer and is reverenced by the liturgy itself as the sublime prerogative of the holy Creative Principle.[1]

Prayer must be simple, wholesome, and powerful. It must be closely related to actuality and not afraid to call things by their names. In prayer we must find our entire life over again. On the other hand, it must be rich in ideas and powerful images, and speak a developed but restrained language ; its construction must be clear and obvious to the simple man, stimulating and refreshing to the man of culture. It must be intimately blended with an erudition which is in nowise obtrusive, but which is rooted in breadth of spiritual outlook and in inward restraint of thought, volition, and emotion.

And that is precisely the way in which the prayer of the liturgy has been formed.

[1] The above remarks must not be misunderstood. Certainly the grace of God is self-sufficient ; neither nature nor the work of man is necessary in order that a soul may be sanctified. God ' can awaken of these stones children to Abraham.' But as a rule He wishes that everything which belongs to man in the way of good, lofty, natural and cultural possessions shall be placed at the disposal of religion and so serve the Kingdom of God. He has interconnected the natural and the supernatural order, and has given natural things a place in the scheme of His supernatural designs. It is the duty of His representative on earth, ecclesiastical authority, to decide how and to what extent these natural means of attaining the supernatural goal are to be utilised.

2

THE FELLOWSHIP OF THE LITURGY

THE liturgy does not say 'I,' but 'We,' unless the particular action which is being performed specifically requires the singular number (*e.g.*, a personal declaration, certain prayers offered by the bishop or the priest in his official capacity, and so on). The liturgy is not celebrated by the individual, but by the body of the faithful. This is not composed merely of the persons who may be present in church; it is not the assembled congregation. On the contrary, it reaches out beyond the bounds of space to embrace all the faithful on earth. Simultaneously it reaches beyond the bounds of time, to this extent, that the body which is praying upon earth knows itself to be at one with those for whom time no longer exists, who, being perfected, exist in Eternity.

Yet this definition does not exhaust the conception of the universality and the all-embracingness which characterise the fellowship of the liturgy. The entity which performs the liturgical actions is not merely the sum total of all individual Catholics. It *does* consist of all these united in one body, but only in so far as this unity is of itself something, apart from the millions which compose it. And that something is the Church.

Here we find an analogy with what happens in the body politic. The State is more than the sum total of citizens, authorities, laws, organisations, and so on. In this con-

nection discussion of the time-honoured question—
whether this higher unity is real or imagined—is beside
the point. In any case, as far as personal perception is
concerned, it does exist. The members of a State are not
only conscious of being parts of a greater whole, but also
of being as it were members of an overlapping, fundamental, living unity.

On an essentially different plane—the supernatural—a
more or less corresponding phenomenon may be witnessed
in the Church. The Church is self-contained, a structure-
system of intricate and invisible vital principles, of means
and ends, of activity and production, of people, organisations, and laws. It does consist of the faithful, then ; but
it is more than the mere body of these, passively held
together by a system of similar convictions and regulations.
The faithful are actively united by a vital and fundamental
principle common to them all. That principle is Christ
Himself ; His life is ours ; we are incorporated in Him ;
we are His Body, *Corpus Christi mysticum*.[1] The active
force which governs this living unity, grafting the individual on to it, granting him a share in its fellowship and
preserving this right for him, is the Holy Ghost.[2] Every
individual Catholic is a cell of this living organism or a
member of this Body.

The individual is made aware of the unity which
comprehends him on many and various occasions, but
chiefly in the liturgy. In it he sees himself face to face
with God, not as an entity, but as a member of this unity.
It is the unity which addresses God ; the individual merely

[1] Cf. Rom. xii. 4 *et seq.* ; 1 Cor. xii. 4 *et seq.* ; Eph., chaps. i.–iv. ;
Col. i. 15 *et seq.*, and elsewhere.
[2] Cf. 1 Cor. xii. 4 *et seq.* ; M. J. Scheeben, *Die Mysterien des Christentums*, pp. 314–508 (Freiburg, 1912).

speaks in it, and it requires of him that he should know and acknowledge that he is a member of it.

It is on the plane of liturgical relations that the individual experiences the meaning of religious fellowship. The individual—provided that he actually desires to take part in the celebration of the liturgy—must realise that it is as a member of the Church that he, and the Church within him, acts and prays; he must know that in this higher unity he is at one with the rest of the faithful, and he must desire to be so.

From this, however, arises a very perceptible difficulty. It is chiefly to be traced to a more common one, concerning the relation between the individual and the community. The religious community, like every other, exacts two things from the individual. The first is a sacrifice, which consists in the renouncement by the individual of everything in him which exists merely for itself and excludes others, while and in so far as he is an active member of the community: he must lay self aside, and live with, and for, others, sacrificing to the community a proportion of his self-sufficiency and independence. In the second place he must produce something; and that something is the widened outlook resulting from his acceptance and assimilation of a more comprehensive scheme of life than his own—that of the community.

This demand will be differently met, according to the disposition of each individual. Perhaps it will be the more impersonal element of spiritual life—the ideas, the ordering of instruments and designs, the objectives, laws and rules, the tasks to be accomplished, the duties and rights, and so on—which first arrests the attention. Both the sacrifice and production indicated above will in such cases assume a more concrete character. The individual has to renounce his own ideas and his own way. He is obliged to subscribe to the ideas and to follow the lead of the liturgy. To it he must surrender his independence ; pray with others, and not alone ; obey, instead of freely disposing of himself ; and stand in the ranks, instead of moving about at his own will and pleasure. It is, furthermore, the task of the individual to apprehend clearly the ideal world of the liturgy. He must shake off the narrow trammels of his own thought, and make his own a far more comprehensive world of ideas : he must go beyond his little personal aims and adopt the educative purpose of the great fellowship of the liturgy. It goes without saying, therefore, that he is obliged to take part in exercises which do not respond to the particular needs of which he is conscious ; that he must ask for things which do not directly concern him ; espouse and plead before God causes which do not affect him personally, and which merely arise out of the needs of the community at large ; he must at times—and this is inevitable in so richly developed a system of symbols, prayer and action—take part in proceedings of which he does not entirely, if at all, understand the significance.

All this is particularly difficult for modern people, who find it so hard to renounce their independence. And yet people who are perfectly ready to play a subordinate part in state and commercial affairs are all the more susceptible and the more passionately reluctant to regulate their spiritual life by dictates other than those of their private and personal requirements. The requirements of the liturgy can be summed up in one word, humility. Humility by renunciation ; that is to say, by the abdication of self-rule and self-sufficiency. And humility by positive action ;

that is to say, by the acceptance of the spiritual principles which the liturgy offers and which far transcend the little world of individual spiritual existence.

The demands of the liturgy's communal life wear a different aspect for the people who are less affected by its concrete and impersonal side. For the latter, the problem of fellowship does not so much consist in the question of how they are to assimilate the universal and, as it were, concrete element, at the same time subordinating themselves to and dovetailing into it. The difficulty rather lies in their being required to divide their existence with other people, to share the intimacy of their inner life, their feeling and willing, with others; and to know that they are united with these others in a higher unity. And by others we mean not one or two neighbours, or a small circle of people, congenial by reason of similar aims or special relations, but with all, even with those who are indifferent, adverse, or even hostilely-minded.

The demand here resolves itself into the breaking down of the barriers which the more sensitive soul sets around its spiritual life. The soul must issue forth from these if it is to go among others and share their existence. Just as in the first case the community was perceived as a great concrete order, in the second it is perceived as a broad tissue of personal affinities, an endless interweaving of living reciprocal relations. The sacrifice required in the first place is that of renouncing the right of self-determination in spiritual activity; in the second, that of renouncing spiritual isolation. There it is a question of subordinating self to a fixed and objective order, here of sharing life in common with other people. There humility is required, here charity and vigorous expansion of self.

There the given spiritual content of the liturgy must be assimilated ; here life must be lived in common with the other members of Christ's Body, their petitions included with one's own, their needs voiced as one's own. There ' We ' is the expression of selfless objectivity ; here it signifies that he who employs it is expanding his inner life in order to include that of others, and to assimilate theirs to his. In the first case, the pride which insists upon independence, and the aggressive intolerance often bred by individual existence, must be overcome, while the entire system of communal aims and ideas must be assimilated ; in the second, the repulsion occasioned by the strangeness of corporate life must be mastered, and the shrinking from self-expansion, and that exclusiveness triumphed over, which leads us to desire only the company of such as we have ourselves chosen and to whom we have voluntarily opened out. Here, too, is required continual spiritual abnegation, a continuous projection of self at the desire of others, and a great and wonderful love which is ready to participate in their life and to make that life its own.

Yet the subordination of self is actually facilitated by a peculiarity inherent in liturgical life itself. It forms at once the complement of and contrast to what has already been discussed. Let us call the disposition manifesting itself in the two forms indicated above, the individualistic. Facing it stands the social disposition, which eagerly and consistently craves for fellowship, and lives in terms of ' We ' just as involuntarily as the former bases itself on the exclusive ' I.' The social disposition will, when it is spiritually active, automatically seek out congenial associates ; and their joint striving towards union will be characterised by a firmness and decision alien to the liturgy. It is sufficient to recall in this connection the systems of spiritual association and fellowship peculiar to certain sects. Here at times the bounds of personality diminish to such an extent that all spiritual reserve is lost, and frequently all external reserve as well. Naturally this description only applies to extreme cases, but it still shows the tendency of the social urge in such dispositions. For this reason people like this will not find all their expectations immediately fulfilled in the liturgy. The fellowship of the liturgy will to them appear frigid and restricted. From which it follows that this fellowship, however complete and genuine it may be, still acts as a check upon unconditional self-surrender. The social urge is opposed by an equally powerful tendency which sees to it that a certain fixed boundary is maintained. The individual is, it is true, a member of the whole—but he is only a member. He is not utterly merged in it ; he is added to it, but in such a way that he throughout remains an entity, existing of himself. This is notably borne out by the fact that the union of the members is not directly accomplished from man to man. It is accomplished by and in their joint aim, goal, and spiritual resting place—God—by their identical creed, sacrifice and sacraments. In the liturgy it is of very rare occurrence that speech and response, and action or gesture are immediately directed from one member of the fellowship to the other.[1] When this does occur, it is generally worth while to observe the great restraint which characterises such communication. It is governed by strict regulations. The individual is never drawn into

[1] This does not apply, of course, to the communication between the hierarchical persons and the faithful. This relation is continual and direct.

contacts which are too extensively direct. He is always free to decide how far he is to get into touch, from the spiritual point of view, with others in that which is common to them all, in God. Take the kiss of peace, for instance ; when it is performed according to the rubric it is a masterly manifestation of restrained and elevated social solidarity.

This is of great importance. It is hardly necessary to point out what would be the infallible consequences of attempting to transmit the consciousness of their fellowship in the liturgy directly from one individual to another. The history of the sects teems with examples bearing on this point. For this reason the liturgy sets strict bounds between individuals. Their union is moderated by a continually watchful sentiment of disparity and by reciprocal reverence. Their fellowship notwithstanding, the one individual can never force his way into the intimacy of the other, never influence the latter's prayers and actions, nor force upon the latter his own characteristics, feelings and perceptions. Their fellowship consists in community of intention, thought and language, in the direction of eyes and heart to the one aim ; it consists in their identical belief, the identical sacrifice which they offer, the Divine Food which nourishes them all alike ; in the one God and Lord Who unites them mystically in Himself. But individuals in their quality of distinct corporeal entities do not among themselves intrude upon each other's inner life.

It is this reserve alone which in the end makes fellowship in the liturgy possible ; but for it the latter would be unendurable. By this reserve again the liturgy keeps all vulgarising elements at a distance. It never allows the soul to feel that it is imprisoned with others, or that its independence and intimacy are threatened with invasion.

From the man of individualistic disposition, then, a sacrifice for the good of the community is required ; from the man of social disposition, submission to the austere restraint which characterises liturgical fellowship. While the former must accustom himself to frequenting the company of his fellows, and must acknowledge that he is only a man among men, the latter must learn to subscribe to the noble, restrained forms which etiquette requires in the House and at the Court of the Divine Majesty.

3

THE STYLE OF THE LITURGY

STYLE is chiefly spoken of in a universal sense. By style we understand those particular characteristics which distinguish every valid and genuine production or organism as such, whether it is a work of art, a personality, a form of society, or anything whatever; it denotes that any given vital principle has found its true and final expression. But this self-expression must be of such a nature that it simultaneously imparts to the individual element a universal significance, reaching far beyond its own particular sphere. For the essence of individuality embraces within itself a second element; it is true that it is particular and unreproducible, but it is at the same time universal, standing in relationship to the other individuals of its kind, and manifesting in its permanent existence traits which are also borne by others. The greater the originality and forcefulness of an individual thing, the greater its capacity of comprehensively revealing the universal essence of its kind,[1] the greater is its significance. Now if a personality, a work of art, or a form of society has, by virtue of its existence and activity, expressed in a convincing manner that which it really is, and if at the same time by its quality

---

[1] The essence of genius, of the man of genius (*e.g.*, of the Saint), and of the really great work or deed consists in this, that it is immeasurably original and yet is still universally applicable to human life.

of specialness it does not merely represent an arbitrary mood, but its relation to a corporate life, then and to that extent it may be said to have style.

In this sense the liturgy undoubtedly has created a style. It is unnecessary to waste further words on the subject.

The conception can, however, be given a narrower sense. Why is it that in front of a Greek temple we are more intensely conscious of style than we are in front of a Gothic cathedral? The inner effect of both these structures is identically powerful and convincing. Each is the perfect expression of a particular type or form of space-perception. Each reveals the individuality of a people, but at the same time affords a profound insight into the human soul and the significance of the world in general. Yet before the temple of Pæstum we are more strongly conscious of style than we are before the cathedrals of Cologne and of Rheims. What is the reason? Why is it that for the uncultured observer Giotto has the more style in comparison with Grünewald, who is without any doubt equally powerful; and the figure of an Egyptian king more than Donatello's wonderful statue of St. John?

In this connection the word *style* has a specialised meaning. It conveys that in the works of art to which reference has been made the individual yields place to the universal. The fortuitous element—determined by place and time, with its significance restricted to certain specific people—is superseded by that which is essentially, or at least more essentially, intended for many times, places and people. The particular is to a great degree absorbed by the universal and ideal. In such works an involved mental or spiritual condition, for instance, which could only have expressed itself in an abstruse utterance or in an unreproducible action, is simplified and reduced to its elements.[1] By this process it is made universally comprehensible. The incalculable ebullition is given a permanent basis. It then becomes easily penetrable and capable of demonstrating in itself the interweaving of cause and effect.[2] The solitary historical event serves to throw into relief the vital significance, universal and unaffected by time, which reposes within it. The figure which appears but once is made to personify characteristics common to the whole of society. The hasty, impetuous movement is restrained and measured. Whereas it was formerly confined to specific relationships or circumstances, it can now to a certain degree be accepted by everyone.[3] Things, materials and instruments are divested of their fortuitous character, their elements revealed, their purpose defined, and their power of expressing certain moods or ideas is heightened.[4] In a word, while one type of art and of life is endeavouring to express that which is special and particular, this other, on the contrary, is striving to hold up to our view that which is universally significant. The latter type of art fashions simple reality, which is always specialised, in such a manner that the ideal and universal comes to the fore ; that is to say, its style is developed and its form is fixed. And so whenever life, with its entanglements and its multiplicity, has been simplified in this way, whenever its inner lawfulness is emphasised and it is raised from the particular to the universal, we are always conscious of style in the narrower sense of the word. Admittedly it is

[1] Cf. the inner life in Ibsen's plays, for instance, with that of Sophoclean tragedy, the ' Ghosts,' perhaps, with ' Œdipus.'
[2] Cf. the line of action adopted by, *e.g.*, Hedda Gabler and Antigone.
[3] Such is the origin of social deportment and of court usage.
[4] Such is the origin of symbols—social, state, religious and otherwise.

difficult to say where style ends and arrangement begins. If the arrangement is too accentuated, if the modelling is carried out according to rules and ideas, and not according to its vital connection with reality, if the production is the result, not of exact observation, but of deliberate planning, then it will be universal only, and therefore lifeless and void.[1] True style, even in its strictest form, still retains the developed faculty of convincing expression. Only that which is living has style; pure thought, and the productions of pure thought, have none.

Now the liturgy—at any rate, as far as the greater part of its range is concerned—has style in the stricter sense of the word. It is not the direct expression of any particular type of spiritual disposition, either in its language and ideas, or in its movements, actions and the materials which it employs. If we compare, for instance, the Sunday Collects with the prayers of an Anselm of Canterbury, or of a Newman; the gestures of the officiating priest with the involuntary movements of the man who fancies himself unobserved while at prayer; the Church's directions on the adornment of the sanctuary, on vestments and altar-vessels, with popular methods of decoration, and of dress on religious occasions; and Gregorian chant with the popular hymn—we shall always find, within the sphere of the liturgy, that the medium of spiritual expression, whether it consists of words, gestures, colours or materials, is to a certain degree divested of its singleness of purpose, intensified, tranquillised, and given universal currency.

Many causes have contributed to this result. For one thing, the passing centuries have continually polished,

[1] It is this which differentiates various classical periods from the classical age.

elaborated and adapted the form of liturgical expression. Then the strongly generalising effect of religious thought must be taken into account. Finally, there is the influence of the Greco-Latin spirit, with its highly significant tendency towards style in the strict sense of the word.

Now if we consider the fact that these quietly constructive forces were at work on the vital form of expression, not of an individual, but of an organic unity, composed of the greatness, exclusiveness and strength of the collective consciousness that is the Catholic Church; if we consider further that the vital formula thus fashioned steadily concentrates its whole attention upon the hereafter, that it aspires from this world to the next, and as a natural result is characterised by eternal, sublime and superhuman traits, then we shall find assembled here all the preliminary conditions essential to the development of a style of great vigour and intensity. If it were capable of doing so anywhere, here above all should develop a living style, spiritual, lofty and exalted. And that is precisely what has happened. If we reflect upon the liturgy as a whole, and upon its important points, not upon the abbreviated form in which it is usually presented, but as it should be, we shall have the good fortune to experience the miracle of a truly mighty style. We shall see and feel that an inner world of immeasurable breadth and depth has created for itself so rich and so ample an expression, and one at the same time so lucid and so universal in form, that its like has never been seen, either before or since.

And it is style in the stricter sense of the word as well —clear in language, measured in movement, severe in its modelling of space, materials, colours and sounds; its ideas, languages, ceremonies and imagery fashioned out of the simple elements of spiritual life; rich, varied and lucid; its force further intensified by the fact that the liturgy employs a classic language, remote from everyday life.

When all these considerations are borne in mind it is easy to understand that the liturgy possesses a tremendously compelling form of expression, which is a school of religious training and development to the Catholic who rightly understands it, and which is bound to appear to the impartial observer as a cultural formation of the most lofty and elevated kind.

It cannot, however, be denied that great difficulties lie in the question of the adaptability of the liturgy to every individual, and more especially to the modern man. The latter wants to find in prayer—particularly if he is of an independent turn of mind—the direct expression of his spiritual condition. Yet in the liturgy he is expected to accept, as the mouthpiece of his inner life, a system of ideas, prayer and action, which is too highly generalised, and, as it were, unsuited to him. It strikes him as being formal and almost meaningless. He is especially sensible of this when he compares the liturgy with the natural outpourings of spontaneous prayer. Liturgical formulas, unlike the language of a person who is spiritually congenial, are not to be grasped straightway without any further mental exertion on the listener's part; liturgical actions have not the same direct appeal as, say, the involuntary movement of understanding on the part of someone who is sympathetic by reason of circumstances and disposition; the emotional impulses of the liturgy do not so readily find an echo as does the spontaneous utterance of the soul. These clear-cut formulas are liable to grate more particularly upon the modern man, so intensely sensitive in everything which affects his scheme of life, who looks for a touch of nature everywhere and listens so attentively for the personal note. He easily tends to consider the idiom of the liturgy as artificial, and its ritual as purely formal. Consequently he will often take refuge in forms of prayer and devotional practices whose spiritual value is far inferior to that of the liturgy, but which seem to have one advantage over the latter—that of contemporary, or, at any rate, of congenial origin.

Those who honestly want to come to grips with this problem in all its bearings should for their own guidance note the way in which the figure of Christ is represented, first in the liturgy, and then in the Gospels. In the latter everything is alive; the reader breathes the air of earth; he sees Jesus of Nazareth walking about the streets and among the people, hears His incomparable and persuasive words, and is aware of the heart-to-heart intercourse between Jesus and His followers. The charm of vivid actuality pervades the historical portrait of Christ. He is so entirely one of us, a real person—Jesus, ' the Carpenter's Son '—Who lived in Nazareth in a certain street, wore certain clothes, and spoke in a certain manner. That is just what the modern man longs for; and he is made happy by the fact that in this actual historical figure is incarnate the living and eternal Godhead, One with the body, so that He is in the fullest sense of the word ' true God and true Man.'

But how differently does the figure of Jesus appear in the liturgy ! There He is the Sovereign Mediator between God and man, the eternal High-Priest, the divine Teacher, the Judge of the living and of the dead; in His Body, hidden in the Eucharist, He mystically unites all the faithful in the great society that is the Church; He is the God-Man, the Word that was made Flesh. The human element, or—involuntarily the theological expression rises to the lips—the Human Nature certainly remains intact, for the battle against Eutyches was not fought in vain; He is truly and wholly human, with a body and soul which have actually lived. But they are now utterly transformed by the Godhead, rapt into the light of eternity, and remote from time and space. He is the Lord, 'sitting at the right hand of the Father,' the mystic Christ living on in His Church.

It will be objected that in the Gospels of the Mass we can still follow the historical life of Jesus in its entirety. That is absolutely true. But if we endeavour to listen more attentively, we shall still find that a particular light is thrown on these narratives by their context. They are a part of the Mass, of the *mysterium magnum*, pervaded by the mystery of sacrifice, an integral part of the structure of the particular Sunday office, current season, or ecclesiastical year, swept along by that powerful straining upwards to the Hereafter which runs through the entire liturgy. In this way the contents of the Gospels, which we hear chanted, and in a foreign language, are in their turn woven into the pattern. Of ourselves we come to consider, not the particular traits which they contain, but their eternal, superhistorical meaning.

Yet by this the liturgy has not—as Protestantism has sometimes accused it of doing—disfigured the Christ of the Gospels. It has not set forth a frigid intellectual conception instead of the living Jesus.

The Gospels themselves, according to the aims and

purpose of the respective Evangelists, stress first one, then another aspect of the personality and activity of Christ. Facing the portrait contained in the first three Gospels, in the Epistles of St. Paul Christ appears as God, mystically living on in His Church and in the souls of those who believe in Him. The Gospel of St. John shows the Word made Flesh, and finally, in the Apocalypse God is made manifest in His eternal splendour. But this does not mean that the historical facts of Christ's human existence are in any way kept back; on the contrary, they are always taken for granted and often purposely emphasised.[1] The liturgy therefore has done nothing that Holy Scripture itself does not do. Without discarding one stroke or trait of the historical figure of Christ, it has, for its own appointed purpose, more strongly stressed the eternal and super-temporal elements of that figure, and for this reason —the liturgy is no mere commemoration of what once existed, but is living and real; it is the enduring life of Jesus Christ in us, and that of the believer in Christ, eternally God and Man.

It is precisely because of this, however, that the difficulty still persists. It is good to make it absolutely clear, since the modern man experiences it more especially. More than one—according to his instinctive impulse—would be content to forego the profoundest knowledge of theology, if as against that it were permitted to him to watch Jesus walking about the streets or to hear the tone in which He addresses a disciple. More than one would be willing to sacrifice the most beautiful liturgical prayer, if in exchange he might meet Christ face to face and speak to Him from the bottom of his heart.

[1] As, for instance, in the beginning of the Gospel of St. John.

Where is the angle to be found from which this difficulty is to be tackled and overcome? It is in the view that it is hardly permissible to play off the spiritual life of the individual, with its purely personal bearing, against the spiritual life of the liturgy, with its generalising bias. They are not mutually contradictory; they should both combine in active co-operation.

When we pray on our own behalf only we approach God from an entirely personal standpoint, precisely as we feel inclined or impelled to do according to our feelings and circumstances. That is our right, and the Church would be the last to wish to deprive us of it. Here we live our own life, and are as it were face to face with God.[1] His Face is turned towards us, as to no one else; He belongs to each one of us. It is this power of being a personal God, ever fresh to each of us, equally patient and attentive to each one's wants, which constitutes the inexhaustible wealth of God. The language which we speak on these occasions suits us entirely, and much of it apparently is suited to us alone. We can use it with confidence because God understands it, and there is no one else who needs to do so.

We are, however, not only individuals, but members of a community as well; we are not merely transitory, but something of us belongs to eternity, and the liturgy takes these elements in us into account. In the liturgy we pray as members of the Church; by it we rise to the sphere which transcends the individual order and is therefore accessible to people of every condition, time, and place.

[1] Even if here, as in the whole range of spiritual things, the Church is our guide. But she is so in a different manner than where the liturgy is concerned.

For this order of things the style of the liturgy—vital, clear, and universally comprehensible—is the only possible one. The reason for this is that any other type of prayer, based upon one particular set of hypotheses or requirements, would undoubtedly prove a totally unsuitable form for a content of different origin. Only a system of life and thought which is truly Catholic—that is to say, actual and universal—is capable of being universally adopted, without violence to the individual. Yet there is still an element of sacrifice involved in such adoption. Each one is bound to strive within himself, and to rise superior to self. Yet in so doing he is not swallowed up by, and lost in, the majority ; on the contrary, he becomes more independent, rich, and versatile.

Both methods of prayer must co-operate. They stand together in a vital and reciprocal relationship. The one derives its light and fruitfulness from the other. In the liturgy the soul learns to move about the wider and more spacious spiritual world. It assimilates—if the comparison is permissible—that freedom and dignified restraint which in human intercourse is acquired by the man who frequents good society, and who limits his self-indulgence by the discipline of time-honoured social usage ; the soul expands and develops in that width of feeling and clearness of form which together constitute the liturgy, just as it does through familiarity and communion with great works of art. In a word, the soul acquires, in the liturgy, the ' grand manner ' of the spiritual life—and that is a thing that cannot be too highly prized. On the other hand, as the Church herself reminds us—and the example of the Orders who live by the liturgy is a proof of this—side by side with the liturgy there must continue to exist that private devotion which provides for the personal requirements of the individual, and to which the soul surrenders itself according to its particular circumstances. From the latter liturgical prayer in its turn derives warmth and local colour.

If private devotion were non-existent, and if the liturgy were the final and exclusive form of spiritual exercise, that exercise might easily degenerate into a frigid formula; but if the liturgy were non-existent—well, our daily observations amply show what would be the consequences, and how fatally they would take effect.

4

THE SYMBOLISM OF THE LITURGY

In the liturgy the faithful are confronted by a new world, rich in types and symbols, which are expressed in terms of ritual, actions, vestments, implements, places, and hours, all of which are highly significant. Out of this the question arises—what is the precise significance of all this as regards the soul's intercourse with God? God is above space; what has He to do with directions as to specific localities? God is above time; what does time, beginning with the liturgical hours and ending with the ecclesiastical year, matter to Him? God is Simplicity; then how is He concerned with specific ritual, actions and instruments? Let us desist from the attempt to enter more fully into the question, and content ourselves with asking: God is a Spirit—can matter therefore have any significance in the soul's intercourse with Him? Is not the intervention of material things bound to pervert and to degrade this intercourse? And even if we admit that man consists of soul and body, that he is not pure spirit, and therefore as a logical conclusion that a material element will always play a certain part in his spiritual life—must we not regard this as a defect against which we must strive? Should it not be the task of all true religion to come to be the ' worship of God in spirit and in truth,' and at least to aim at, if not to succeed in, eliminating the bodily and material element as far as possible?

This question penetrates deeply into the essence and nature of the liturgy.

What meaning has matter—regarded as the medium of spiritual receptivity and utterance, of spiritual impression and expression—for us ?

The question depends upon the manner in which the Ego, within its bodily-spiritual personality, experiences the relationship between body and soul.[1] There exists a peculiar form of this self-experience, in which the boundary between the ' spiritual ' and the ' bodily ' or ' physical ' is sharply defined. In such cases the spiritual plane appears as entirely self-contained, lying within—or perhaps it would be better to say beyond—the physical plane, and having little or nothing to do with the latter. The two planes—spiritual and physical—are felt to be two distinct orders, lying closely adjacent, between which communication certainly takes place ; but communication of such a nature that it rather appears as a transposition from the one into the other, than as the direct co-operation of both. Such is the frame of mind which has probably drawn its conception of the external world from Leibniz's theory of monads, and its conception of the soul from the teaching of psycho-physical parallelism.

It is obvious that people who favour such a system of thought will only attach a more or less fortuitous significance to the relationship between the physical and the spiritual. The latter, they consider, is intimately bound up with the former, and is also in need of it, but as far as the life of the soul proper is concerned, the physical has no importance ; it merely appears to encumber and to

[1] The more precise discussion of the question belongs to the domain, as yet but little explored, of typological psychology.

degrade spiritual activity. The soul strives to attain its goal—that is to say, truth, the moral impulse, God, and the Divine—by purely spiritual means. Even when such people know that this endeavour cannot possibly succeed, they still exert themselves to approach to the purely spiritual at least as nearly as they can. To them the physical is an alloy, an innate imperfection, of which they endeavour to rid themselves. They may perhaps credit it with a limited external significance, and look upon it as an aid to the elucidation of the spiritual, as an illustration, or as an allegory; but they are all the time conscious that they are making what is actually an inadmissible concession. Moreover, the physical does not appeal to them as a medium of vividly expressing their inner life. They scarcely even feel the need of expressing that life in a tangible manner; for them the spiritual is self-sufficing, or else it can express itself in a straightforward moral action and in a simply uttered word.

People of such a turn of mind will inevitably have great difficulties to face in the liturgy.[1] Somewhat naturally, they gravitate towards a strictly spiritual form of devotion, which aims at suppressing the physical or material element and at shaping its external manifestations in as plain and homely a manner as possible; it prizes the simple word as the most spiritual medium of communication.

Facing these, and in contrast with them, are people of a different mental constitution. For them, the spiritual and the physical are inextricably jumbled together[2]; they

[1] This disposition does not, of course, actually exist in the extreme form portrayed here any more than does that which is described later. We are concerned, however, with giving an account of such conditions in the abstract and not in detail.

[2] It need hardly be said that no intention exists of discussing in this

incline to amalgamate the two. While the former type of disposition labours to separate the physical and the spiritual spheres, the latter endeavours to unite them. People like this are prone to look upon the soul merely as the lining of the body, and upon the body as the outside, in some sort the condensation or materialisation, of the spirit within. They interpret spiritual elements in terms of physical conditions or movements, and directly perceive every material action as a spiritual experience. They extend their conviction of the essential oneness of the soul and the body beyond the province of the individual personality, and include external things within its sphere of operation. As they frequently tend to regard externals as the manifestation of spiritual elements, they are also capable of utilising them as a means of expressing their own innerness. They see this expressed in various substances, in clothing, in social formations, and in Nature, while their inner struggles are reflected even in conditions, desires, and conflicts which are universal.[1]

Of the two types of spiritual character, the second at the first glance would seem to correspond the more closely to the nature of the liturgy. It is far more susceptible to the power of expression proper to liturgical action and materials, and can the more readily apply these external phenomena to the expression of its own inner life. Yet in the liturgy it has to face problems and difficulties all its own.

People who perceive the physical or material and the

connection the real relationship of soul and body. We are concerned with describing the manner in which this relationship is felt and interiorly experienced. It is not a question of metaphysics, but merely of descriptive psychology.

[1] Cf., for instance, the feeling of the Romantics for Nature.

spiritual as inextricably mingled find it hard to confine the manifestations of the individual soul to set forms of expression, and to adhere strictly to the clearly defined significance of the formulas, actions and instruments employed in such expression. They conceive the inner life as being in a perpetual state of flux. They cannot create definite and clearly outlined forms of expression, because they are incapable of separating spiritual from physical or material objects. They find it equally difficult to distinguish clearly the specific substance behind the given forms of expression; they will always give it a fresh interpretation according to varying circumstances.[1]

In other words, in spite of the close relationship which in this case exists between the physical and the spiritual, such people lack the power of welding certain spiritual contents to certain external forms, which together will constitute either the expression of their inner selves or a receptacle for an extraneous content. That is to say, they lack one of the ingredients essential to the creation of symbols. The other type of people do not succeed any better, because they fail to realise how vital the relationship is between the spiritual and the physical. They are perfectly capable of differentiating and of delimiting the boundaries between the two, but they do this to such an extent that they lose all sense of cohesion. The second type possess a sense of cohesion, and with them the inner content issues directly into the external form. But they lack discrimination and objectiveness. Both—the sense

[1] Hence the tendency of people like this to forsake the Church, with her clear and unequivocal formulas, and to turn to Nature, there to seek an outlet for their vague and fluctuating emotions and to win from her the stimulus that suits them.

of cohesion and the power of discrimination—are essential to the creation of a symbol.

A symbol may be said to originate when that which is interior and spiritual finds expression in that which is exterior and material. But it does not originate when [1] a spiritual element is by general consent coupled with a material substance, as, for instance, the image of the scales with the idea of Justice. Rather must the spiritual element transpose itself into material terms because it is vital and essential that it should do so. Thus the body is the natural emblem of the soul, and a spontaneous physical movement will typify a spiritual event. The symbol proper is circumscribed; and it may be further distinguished by the total inability of the form selected as a medium of expression to represent anything else whatever. It must be expressed in clear and precise terms and therefore, when it has fulfilled the usual conditions, must be universally comprehensible. A genuine symbol is occasioned by the spontaneous expression of an actual and particular spiritual condition. But at the same time, like works of art, it must rise above the purely individual plane. It must not merely express isolated spiritual elements, but deal with life and the soul in the abstract.

Consequently when a symbol has been created, it often enjoys widespread currency and becomes universally comprehensible and significant. The auspicious collaboration of both the types of temperament outlined above is essential to the creation of a symbol, in which the spiritual and the physical elements must be united in perfect harmony. At the same time it is the task of the spiritual element to watch over and determine every stroke of the

[1] As in allegory.

modelling, to sort and sift with a sure hand, to measure off and weigh together delicately and discreetly, in order that the given matter may be given its corresponding and appropriate form. The more clearly and completely a spiritual content is cast in its material mould, the more valuable is the symbol thus produced, and the more worthy it is of its name, because it then loses its connection with the solitary incident which occasioned it and becomes a universal possession. The greater the depth of life from which it has sprung, and the greater the degree of clarity and of conviction which has contributed to its formation, the more true this is in proportion.

The power of symbol-building was at work, for instance, when the fundamental rules governing social intercourse were laid down. From it are derived those forms by which one person signifies to another interest or reverence, in which are externally expressed the inward happenings of civil and political life, and the like. Further —and in this connection it is specially significant—it is the origin of those gestures which convey a spiritual meaning ; the man who is moved by emotion will kneel, bow, clasp his hands or impose them, stretch forth his arms, strike his breast, make an offering of something, and so on. These elementary gestures are capable of richer development and expansion, or else of amalgamation. They are the source of the manifold ritual actions, such as the kiss of peace or the blessing. Or it may be that certain ideas are expressed in corresponding movements, thus belief in the mystery of absolution is shown by the Sign of the Cross. Finally, a whole series of such movements may be co-ordinated. This gives rise to religious action by which a richly developed spiritual element—*e.g.*, a sacrifice—succeeds in attaining external and symbolic expression. It is when that form of self-experience which has been described above is extended to objects which lie without the personal province, that the material concrete factor enters into the symbol. Material objects are used to reinforce the expressiveness of the body and its movements, and at the same time form an extension of the permanent bodily powers. Thus, for instance, in a sacrifice the victim is offered, not only by the hands, but in a vessel or dish. The smooth surface of the dish emphasises the expressive motion of the hand; it forms a wide and open plane, displayed before the Godhead, and throwing into powerful relief the upward straining line of the arm. Or again, as it rises, the smoke of the incense enhances the aspiration expressed by the upturned hands and gaze of those who are at prayer. The candle, with its slender, soaring, tapering column tipped with flame, and consuming itself as it burns, typifies the idea of sacrifice, which is voluntarily offered in lofty spiritual serenity.

Both the before-mentioned types of temperament co-operate in the creation of symbols. The one, with its apprehension of the affinity between the spiritual and the physical, provides the material for the primary hypothesis essential to the creation of the symbol. The other, by its power of distinction and its objectiveness, brings to the symbol lucidity and form. They both, however, find in the liturgy the problems peculiar to their temperament. But because they have shared together in the creation of the liturgical symbol, both are capable of overcoming these difficulties as soon, that is, as they are at least in some way convinced of the binding value of the liturgy.

The former type, then, must abandon their exaggerated

spirituality, admit the existence of the relationship between the spiritual and the physical, and freely avail themselves of the wealth of liturgical symbolism. They must give up their reserve and the Puritanism which prompts them to oppose the expression of the spiritual in material terms, and must instead take the latter as a medium of lively expression. This will add a new warmth and depth to their emotional and spiritual experience.

The latter type must endeavour to stem their extravagance of sensation, and to bind the vague and ephemeral elements into clear-cut forms. It is of the highest importance that they should realise that the liturgy is entirely free from any subjection to matter,[1] and that all the natural elements in the liturgy (cf. what has been previously said concerning its style) are entirely re-cast as ritual forms. So for people of this type the symbolising power of the liturgy becomes a school of measure and of spiritual restraint.

The people who really live by the liturgy will come to learn that the bodily movements, the actions, and the material objects which it employs are all of the highest significance. It offers great opportunities of expression, of knowledge, and of spiritual experience ; it is emancipating in its action, and capable of presenting a truth far more strongly and convincingly than can the mere word of mouth.

---

[1] Such as is found in Nature-religions, for instance, which are directly derived from Nature herself, from the forest, the sea, etc. The liturgy, on the contrary, is entirely designed by human hands. It would be extremely interesting to investigate in a detailed manner the transformation of natural things, shapes and sounds into ritual objects through the agency of the liturgy.

5

THE PLAYFULNESS OF THE LITURGY

GRAVE and earnest people, who make the knowledge of truth their whole aim, see moral problems in everything, and seek for a definite purpose everywhere, tend to experience a peculiar difficulty where the liturgy is concerned.[1] They incline to regard it as being to a certain extent aimless, as superfluous pageantry of a needlessly complicated and artificial character. They are affronted by the scrupulously exact instructions which the liturgy gives on correct procedure, on the right direction in which to turn, on the pitch of the voice, and so on. What is the use of it all ? The essential part of Holy Mass—the action of Sacrifice and the divine Banquet—could be so easily consummated. Why, then, the need for the solemn institution of the priestly office ? The necessary consecration could be so simply accomplished in so few words, and the sacraments so straightforwardly administered—what is the reason of all the prayers and ceremonies ? The liturgy tends to strike people of this turn of mind as—to use the words which are really most appropriate—trifling and theatrical.

The question is a serious one. It does not occur to everyone, but in the people whom it does affect it is a sign

[1] In what follows the writer must beg the reader not to weigh isolated words and phrases. The matter under consideration is vague and intangible, and not easy to put into words. The writer can only be sure of not being misunderstood if the reader considers the chapter and the general train of thought as a whole.

of the mental attitude which concentrates on and pursues that which is essential. It appears to be principally connected with the question of purpose.

That which we call purpose is, in the true sense of the word, the distributive, organising principle which subordinates actions or objects to other actions or objects, so that the one is directed towards the other, and one exists for the sake of the other. That which is subordinate, the means, is only significant in so far as it is capable of serving that which is superior, the end. The purpose does not infuse a spiritual value into its medium ; it uses it as a passage to something else, a thoroughfare merely ; aim and fulcrum alike reside in the former. From this point of view, every instrument has to prove in the first place whether, and in the second to what extent, it is fitted to accomplish the purpose for which it is employed. This proof will primarily be headed by the endeavour to eliminate from the instrument all the non-essential, unimportant, and superfluous elements. It is a scientific principle that an end should be attained with the minimum expenditure of energy, time, and material. A certain restless energy, an indifference to the cost involved, and accuracy in going to the point, characterise the corresponding turn of mind.

A disposition like this is, on the whole, both appropriate and necessary to life, giving it earnestness and fixity of purpose. It also takes reality into consideration, to the extent of viewing everything from the standpoint of purpose. Many pursuits and professions can be shown to have their origin almost entirely in the idea of purpose. Yet no phenomenon can be entirely, and many can be, to a minor degree only, comprehended in this category. Or, to put it more plainly, that which gives objects and events their right to existence, and justifies their individuality, is in many cases not the sole, and in others not even the primary reason for their usefulness. Are flowers and leaves useful ? Of course ; they are the vital organs of plants. Yet because of this, they are not tied down to any particular form, colour, or smell. Then what, upon the whole, is the use of the extravagance of shapes, colours and scents, in Nature ? To what purpose the multiplicity of species ? Things could be so much more simple. Nature could be entirely filled with animate beings, and they could thrive and progress in a far quicker and more suitable manner. The indiscriminate application to Nature of the idea of purpose is, however, open to objection. To go to the root of the matter, what is the object of this or that plant, and of this or that animal, existing at all ? Is it in order to afford nourishment to some other plant or animal ? Of course not. Measured merely by the standard of apparent and external utility, there is a great deal in Nature which is only partially, and nothing which is wholly and entirely, intended for a purpose, or, better still, purpose*ful*. Indeed, considered in this light, a great deal is purposeless. In a mechanical structure—a machine, say, or a bridge— everything has a purpose ; and the same thing applies to business enterprises or to the government of a State ; yet even where these phenomena are concerned, the idea of purpose is not far-reaching enough to give an adequate reply to the query, whence springs their right to existence ?

If we want to do justice to the whole question, we must shift our angle of vision. The conception of purpose regards an object's centre of gravity as existing outside that object, seeing it lie instead in the transition to further movement, *i.e.*, that towards the goal which the object provides. But every object is to a certain extent, and many are entirely, self-sufficient and an end in itself—if, that is, the conception can be applied at all in this extensive sense. The conception of meaning is more adaptable. Objects which have no purpose in the strict sense of the term have a meaning. This meaning is not realised by their extraneous effect or by the contribution which they make to the stability or the modification of another object, but their significance consists in being what they are. Measured by the strict sense of the word, they are purposeless, but still full of meaning.

Purpose and meaning are the two aspects of the fact that an existent principle possesses the motive for, and the right to, its own essence and existence. An object regarded from the point of view of purpose is seen to dovetail into an order of things which comprehends both it and more beyond it ; from the standpoint of meaning, it is seen to be based upon itself.

Now what is the meaning of that which exists ? That it should exist and should be the image of God the Everlasting. And what is the meaning of that which is alive ? That it should live, bring forth its essence, and bloom as a natural manifestation of the living God.

This is true of Nature. It is also true of the life of the soul. Has science an aim or an object in the real sense of the word ? No. Pragmatism is trying to foist one upon it. It insists that the aim of science is to better humanity and to improve it from the moral point of view. Yet this constitutes a failure to appreciate the independent value of knowledge. Knowledge has no aim, but it has a meaning, and one that is rooted in itself—truth. The legislative activity of Parliament, for instance, has an end in view; it is intended to bring about a certain agreed result in the life of the State. Jurisprudence, on the contrary, has no object; it merely indicates where truth lies in questions of law. The same thing applies to all real science. According to its nature, it is either the knowledge of truth or the service of truth, but nothing else. Has art any aim or purpose ? No, it has not. If it had, we should be obliged to conclude that art exists in order to provide a living for artists, or else, as the eighteenth century German thinkers of the *Aufklärung*—the 'age of enlightenment'—considered, it is intended to offer concrete examples of intelligent views and to inculcate virtue. This is absolutely untrue. The work of art has no purpose, but it has a meaning—' *ut sit* '—that it should exist, and that it should clothe in clear and genuine form the essence of things and the inner life of the human artist. It is merely to be ' *splendor veritatis*,' the glory of truth.

When life lacks the austere guidance of the sense of purpose it degenerates into pseudo-æstheticism. But when it is forced into the rigid framework that is the purely purposeful conception of the world, it droops and perishes. The two conceptions are interdependent. Purpose is the goal of all effort, labour and organisation, meaning is the essence of existence, of flourishing, ripening life. Purpose and meaning, effort and growth, activity and production, organisation and creation—these are the two poles of existence.

The life of the Universal Church is also organised on these lines. In the first place, there is the whole tremendous system of purposes incorporated in the Canon Law, and in the constitution and government of the Church. Here we find every means directed to the one end, that of keeping in motion the great machinery of ecclesiastical government. The first-mentioned point of view will decide whether adjustment or modification best serves the collective purpose, and whether the latter is attained with the least possible expenditure of time and energy.[1] The scheme of labour must be arranged and controlled by a strictly practical spirit.

The Church, however, has another side. It embraces a sphere which is in a special sense free from purpose. And that is the liturgy. The latter certainly comprehends a whole system of aims and purposes, as well as the instruments to accomplish them. It is the business of the Sacraments to act as the channels of certain graces. This mediation, however, is easily and quickly accomplished when the necessary conditions are present. The administration of the Sacraments is an example of a liturgical action which is strictly confined to the one object. Of course, it can be said of the liturgy, as of every action and every prayer which it contains, that it is directed towards the providing of spiritual instruction. This is perfectly true. But the liturgy has no thought-out, deliberate, detailed plan of instruction. In order to sense the difference it is sufficient to compare a week of the ecclesiastical year with the Spiritual Exercises of St. Ignatius. In the latter every element is determined by deliberate choice, everything is directed towards the production of a certain spiritual and didactic result; each exercise, each prayer,

[1] Even when the Church is considered from its other aspect, that of a Divine work of art. Yet the former conception is bound to recur in this connection.

even the way in which the hours of repose are passed, all aim at the one thing, the conversion of the will. It is not so with the liturgy. The fact that the latter has no place in the Spiritual Exercises is a proof of this.[1] The liturgy wishes to teach, but not by means of an artificial system of aim-conscious educational influences ; it simply creates an entire spiritual world in which the soul can live according to the requirements of its nature. The difference resembles that which exists between a gymnasium, in which every detail of the apparatus and every exercise aims at a calculated effect, and the open woods and fields. In the first everything is consciously directed towards discipline and development, in the second life is lived with Nature, and internal growth takes place in her. The liturgy creates a universe brimming with fruitful spiritual life, and allows the soul to wander about in it at will and to develop itself there. The abundance of prayers, ideas, and actions, and the whole arrangement of the calendar are incomprehensible when they are measured by the objective standard of strict suitability for a purpose. The liturgy has no purpose, or, at least, it cannot be considered from the standpoint of purpose. It is not a means which is adapted to attain a certain end—it is an end in itself. This fact is important, because if we overlook it, we labour to find all kinds of didactic purposes in the liturgy which may certainly be stowed away somewhere, but are not actually evident.

When the liturgy is rightly regarded, it cannot be said to have a purpose, because it does not exist for the sake of humanity, but for the sake of God. In the liturgy man is

[1] The Benedictines give it one, but do so in an obviously different system of spiritual exercises to that conceived by St. Ignatius.

no longer concerned with himself; his gaze is directed towards God. In it man is not so much intended to edify himself as to contemplate God's majesty. The liturgy means that the soul exists in God's presence, originates in Him, lives in a world of divine realities, truths, mysteries and symbols, and really lives its true, characteristic and fruitful life.[1]

There are two very profound passages in Holy Scripture, which are quite decisive on the point. One is found in the description of Ezekiel's vision.[2] Let us consider the flaming Cherubim, who 'every one of them went straight forward, whither the impulse of the Spirit was to go . . ., and they turned not when they went . . ., ran and returned like flashes of lightning . . ., went . . . and stood . . . and were lifted up from the earth . . ., the noise of their wings was like the noise of many waters . . ., and when they stood, their wings were let down.' How 'aimless' they are ! How discouraging for the zealous partisans of reasonable suitability for a purpose ! They are only pure motion, powerful and splendid, acting according to the direction of the Spirit, desiring nothing save to express Its inner drift and Its interior glow and force. They are the living image of the liturgy.

In the second passage it is Eternal Wisdom which speaks : 'I was with Him, forming all things, and was delighted every day, playing before Him at all times, playing in the world. . . .'[3]

---

[1] The fact that the liturgy moralises so little is consistent with this conception. In the liturgy the soul forms itself, not by means of deliberate teaching and the exercise of virtue, but by the fact that it exists in the light of eternal Truth, and is naturally and supernaturally robust.

[2] Ezekiel i. 4 *et seq.*, especially 12, 17, 20, 24, and x. 9 *et seq.*

[3] Proverbs viii. 30, 31.

This is conclusive. It is the delight of the Eternal Father that Wisdom (the Son, the perfect Fullness of Truth) should pour out Its eternal essence before Him in all Its ineffable splendour, without any ' purpose '—for what purpose should It have ?—but full of decisive meaning, in pure and vocal happiness ; the Son ' plays ' before the Father.

Such is the life of the highest beings, the angels, who, without a purpose and as the Spirit stirs them, move before God, and are a mystic diversion and a living song before Him.

In the earthly sphere there are two phenomena which tend in the same direction : the play of the child and the creation of the artist.

The child, when it plays, does not aim at anything. It has no purpose. It does not want to do anything but to exercise its youthful powers, pour forth its life in an aimless series of movements, words and actions, and by this to develop and to realise itself more fully ; all of which is purposeless, but full of meaning nevertheless, the significance lying in the unchecked revelation of this youthful life in thoughts and words and movements and actions, in the capture and expression of its nature, and in the fact of its existence. And because it does not aim at anything in particular, because it streams unbroken and spontaneously forth, its utterance will be harmonious, its form clear and fine ; its expression will of itself become picture and dance, rhyme, melody and song. That is what play means ; it is life, pouring itself forth without an aim, seizing upon riches from its own abundant store, significant through the fact of its existence. It will be beautiful, too, if it is left to itself, and if no futile advice and pedagogic attempts at enlightenment foist upon it a host of aims and purposes, thus denaturising it.

Yet, as life progresses, conflicts ensue, and it appears to grow ugly and discordant. Man sets before himself what he wants to do and what he should do, and tries to realise this in his life. But in the course of these endeavours he learns that many obstacles stand in his way, and he perceives that it is very seldom that he can attain his ideal.

It is in a different order, in the imaginary sphere of representation, that man tries to reconcile the contradiction between that which he wishes to be and that which he is. In art he tries to harmonise the ideal and actuality, that which he ought to be and that which he is, the soul within and nature without, the body and the soul. Such are the visions of art. It has no didactic aims, then ; it is not intended to inculcate certain truths and virtues. A true artist has never had such an end in view. In art, he desires to do nothing but to overcome the discord to which we have referred, and to express in the sphere of representation the higher life of which he stands in need, and to which in actuality he has only approximately attained. The artist merely wants to give life to his being and its longings, to give external form to the inner truth. And people who contemplate a work of art should not expect anything of it but that they should be able to linger before it, moving freely, becoming conscious of their own better nature, and sensing the fulfilment of their most intimate longings. But they should not reason and chop logic, or look for instruction and good advice from it.

The liturgy offers something higher. In it man, with the aid of grace, is given the opportunity of realising his fundamental essence, of really becoming that which according to his divine destiny he should be and longs to be, a child of God. In the liturgy he is to go ' unto God, Who giveth joy to his youth.' [1] All this is, of course, on the supernatural plane, but at the same time it corresponds to the same degree to the inner needs of man's nature. Because the life of the liturgy is higher than that to which customary reality gives both the opportunity and form of expression, it adopts suitable forms and methods from that sphere in which alone they are to be found, that is to say, from art. It speaks measuredly and melodiously ; it employs formal, rhythmic gestures ; it is clothed in colours and garments foreign to everyday life ; it is carried out in places and at hours which have been co-ordinated and systematised according to sublimer laws than ours. It is in the highest sense the life of a child, in which everything is picture, melody and song.

Such is the wonderful fact which the liturgy demonstrates ; it unites art and reality in a supernatural childhood before God. That which formerly existed in the world of unreality only, and was rendered in art as the expression of mature human life, has here become reality. These forms are the vital expression of real and frankly supernatural life. But this has one thing in common with the play of the child and the life of art—it has no purpose, but it is full of profound meaning. It is not work, but play. To be at play, or to fashion a work of art in God's sight—not to create, but to exist—such is the essence of the liturgy. From this is derived its sublime mingling of profound earnestness and divine joyfulness. The fact that the liturgy gives a thousand strict and careful directions on the quality of the language, gestures, colours,

[1] Entrance prayer of the Mass.

garments and instruments which it employs, can only be understood by those who are able to take art and play seriously. Have you ever noticed how gravely children draw up the rules of their games, on the form of the melody, the position of the hands, the meaning of this stick and that tree ? It is for the sake of the silly people who may not grasp their meaning and who will persist in seeing the justification of an action or object only in its obvious purpose. Have you ever read of or even experienced the deadly earnestness with which the artist-vassal labours for art, his lord ? Of his sufferings on the score of language ? Or of what an overweening mistress form is ? And all this for something that has no aim or purpose ! No, art does not bother about aims. Does anyone honestly believe that the artist would take upon himself the thousand anxieties and feverish perplexities incident to creation if he intended to do nothing with his work but to teach the spectator a lesson, which he could just as well express in a couple of facile phrases, or one or two historical examples, or a few well-taken photographs ? The only answer to this can be an emphatic negative. Being an artist means wrestling with the expression of the hidden life of man, avowedly in order that it may be given existence ; nothing more. It is the image of the Divine creation, of which it is said that it has made things ' *ut sint.*'

The liturgy does the same thing. It too, with endless care, with all the seriousness of the child and the strict conscientiousness of the great artist, has toiled to express in a thousand forms the sacred, God-given life of the soul to no other purpose than that the soul may therein have its existence and live its life. The liturgy has laid down the serious rules of the sacred game which the soul plays before God. And, if we are desirous of touching bottom in this mystery, it is the Spirit of fire and of holy discipline ' Who has knowledge of the world ' [1]—the Holy Ghost— Who has ordained the game which the Eternal Wisdom plays before the Heavenly Father in the Church, Its kingdom on earth. And ' Its delight ' is in this way ' to be with the children of men.'

Only those who are not scandalised by this understand what the liturgy means. From the very first every type of rationalism has turned against it. The practice of the liturgy means that by the help of grace, under the guidance of the Church, we grow into living works of art before God, with no other aim or purpose than that of living and existing in His sight; it means fulfilling God's word and ' becoming as little children '; it means foregoing maturity with all its purposefulness, and confining oneself to play, as David did when he danced before the Ark. It may, of course, happen that those extremely clever people, who merely from being grown-up have lost all spiritual youth and spontaneity, will misunderstand this and jibe at it. David probably had to face the derision of Michal.

It is in this very aspect of the liturgy that its didactic aim is to be found, that of teaching the soul not to see purposes everywhere, not to be too conscious of the end it wishes to attain, not to be desirous of being over-clever and grown-up, but to understand simplicity in life. The soul must learn to abandon, at least in prayer, the restlessness of purposeful activity; it must learn to waste time for the sake of God, and to be prepared for the sacred game with sayings and thoughts and gestures, without always immediately asking ' why? ' and ' wherefore? '

Responsory at Terce, Pentecost.

It must learn not to be continually yearning to *do* something, to attack something, to accomplish something useful, but to play the divinely ordained game of the liturgy in liberty and beauty and holy joy before God.

In the end, eternal life will be its fulfilment. Will the people who do not understand the liturgy be pleased to find that the heavenly consummation is an eternal song of praise? Will they not rather associate themselves with those other industrious people who consider that such an eternity will be both boring and unprofitable?

6

THE SERIOUSNESS OF THE LITURGY

THE liturgy is art, translated into terms of life. Sensitive people clearly recognise its wealth of expression, its symmetry of form, and its delicate sense of proportion. As a result, such people are in danger of appreciating the Church's worship merely for the sake of its æsthetic value. It is on the whole understandable that poetic literature should apprehend the liturgy from its artistic side. It is a more serious matter when this is so emphatically stressed in writings which are particularly dedicated to liturgical worship. It is sufficient for our purpose to recall valuable works such as Staudenmaier's *Geist des Christentums*, or many of J. K. Huysman's books, *L'Oblat*, for instance. The present writer is anxious that this little work should not gravitate, however unconsciously, in the same direction. For this reason, in the chapter which has been begun, the question will be more closely examined.

It is an incontrovertible proposition that people who consider a work of art merely from the artistic point of view do it an injustice. Its significance as a composition can only be fully estimated when it is viewed in connection with the whole of life. A work of art is in less danger from the logician or the moral philosopher pure and simple, because they stand in no particular relation to it. Deadly destructive to the work of art, however, is the purely artistic perception of the æsthete—both word and matter being taken in the worst and most extreme sense which they have possessed since, for instance, Oscar Wilde.

Still more does this hold good when it is a question, not of the representation of a work of art, but of actual people, and even of that tremendous unity—the *Opus Dei*, that is the liturgy—in which the Creator-Artist, the Holy Ghost, has garnered and expressed the whole fulness of reality and of creative art. Æsthetes are everywhere looked upon as unwelcome guests, as drones and as parasites sponging on life, but nowhere are they more deserving of anger and contempt than in the sphere of sacred things. The careworn man who seeks nothing at Mass but the fulfilment of the service which he owes to his God ; the busy woman, who comes to be a little lightened of her burden ; the many people who, barren of feeling and perceiving nothing of the beauty and splendour of word and sound which surrounds them, but merely seek strength for their daily toil—all these penetrate far more deeply into the essence of the liturgy than does the connoisseur who is busy savouring the contrast between the austere beauty of a Preface and the melodiousness of a Gradual.

All of which impels us to the fundamental question, what is the importance of beauty in relation to the entire liturgical scheme ?

First, however, a slight but necessary digression. We have already seen that the Church's life functions in two directions. On the one side there exists an active communal life, a tremendous driving force of systematically directed activities, which, however, coalesce in the many-membered but strongly centralised organisation. Such a unity alike presupposes and manifests power. But what is the purpose of power in the spiritual sphere?

This query deeply concerns every one of us, each according to his disposition. For the one, it is a question of satisfying himself as to the truth of the axiom that every type of society, including the spiritual, needs power if it is to subsist. The truth of this does not degrade the ideal, even if it ranks power next in order to doctrine, exhortation, and organisation. This external power must not of course be allowed to usurp the place of truth and of justice, nor permitted to influence convictions. Where, however, a religion is concerned which does not confine itself to presenting ideals and opinions, but undertakes the moulding and adapting of human entities on behalf of the Kingdom of God, there power is necessary. It is this which adapts a truth, or a spiritual or ethical system, to the needs of actual existence.

But if there are people who find it hard to bear that things like justice and power should be named in the same breath with such intimate matters as religious convictions and spiritual life, there are others who are entirely differently constituted. Upon such people a tremendous force like the Catholic Church produces so direct an effect that they easily forget the real significance of such power. It is merely a means to an end. It is a tool, used to carve the Kingdom of God from the raw material of the world; it is the servant of Divine truth and grace. If an attempt were to be made to constitute a form of spiritual society without a powerful discipline, it would inevitably dissolve into fleeting shadows. But if power, the servant, were to be promoted to the position of master, the means to that of the end, the tool to that of the guiding hand, religion would then be stifled by despotism and its consequence, slavery.

Somewhat analogous to the position of power in the Church's active life is that of beauty in relation to her contemplative side. The Church not only exists for a purpose, but she is of herself significant, viewed from her other aspect of art transformed into life—or, better still, in the process of transformation. For that is what the Church is in the liturgy.

The preceding chapter endeavoured to demonstrate that artistic self-sufficiency is actually compatible with the liturgy. Only a sophist could argue that the justification of a form of life resides exclusively in its manifest purposes. On the other hand, one must not forget as well that artistic worth—beauty—is as dangerous to the susceptible person as is power in the corresponding sphere of active communal life. The danger inherent in the idea of power is only to be overcome by those who are clear about its nature and the method of employing it. Similarly, only those who force their way into perception of its import can break free from the illusive spell of beauty.

Apart from this stands the question, whence a spiritual value derives its currency, whether from itself or from an extraneous superior value? Associated with it, but entirely distinct, is the second question, as to the quality of the relation which exists between one value which is admittedly based upon itself and other independent values. The first question endeavours to trace one value back to another, *e.g.*, the validity of the administration of justice to justice in the abstract. The second investigates the existence, between two values of equal validity, of a determinate order which may not be inverted.

Truth is of itself a value, because it is truth, justice because it is justice, and beauty because and in so far as it is beauty. No one of these qualities can derive its validity from another, but only from itself.[1] The most profound and true thought does not make a work beautiful, and the best intentions of the artist avail as little, if his creation, in addition to a concrete, vivid and robust form, has not—in a word—beauty. Beauty as such is valid of itself, entirely independent of truth and other values. An object or a work of art is beautiful, when its inner essence and significance find perfect expression in its existence. This perfection of expression embraces the fact of beauty, and is its accepted form of currency. Beauty means that the essence of an object or action has, from the first moment of its existence and from the innermost depths of its being, formulated its relation to the universe and to the spiritual world; that this interior formation, from which has developed a phenomenon susceptible of expression, has resolved upon symbolic unity; that everything is said which should be said, and no more; that the essential form is attained, and no other; that in it there is nothing that is lifeless and empty, but everything that is vivid and animated; that every sound, every word, every surface, shade and movement, emanates from within, contributes to the expression of the whole, and is associated with the rest in a seamless, organic unity. Beauty is the full, clear and inevitable expression of the inner truth in the external manifestation. '*Pulchritudo est splendor veritatis*'—'*est species boni*,' says ancient philosophy, 'beauty is the

---

[1] We are not concerned here with the question if and how all forms of validity ultimately go back to an ultimately valid Absolute, *i.e.*, to God.

splendid perfection which dwells in the revelation of essential truth and goodness.'

Beauty, therefore, is an independent value; it is not truth and not goodness, nor can it be derived from them. And yet it stands in the closest relation to these other values. As we have already remarked, in order that beauty may be made manifest, something must exist which will reveal itself externally; there must be an essential truth which compels utterance, or an event which will out. Pride of place, therefore, though not of rank or worth, belongs, not to beauty, but to truth. Although this applies incontestably to life as a whole, and to the fundamentals of art as well, it will perhaps be difficult for the artist to accept without demur.

'Beauty is the splendour of truth,' says scholastic philosophy. To us moderns this sounds somewhat frigid and superficially dogmatic. But if we remember that this axiom was held and taught by men who were incomparable constructive thinkers, who conceived ideas, framed syllogisms, and established systems, which still tower over others like vast cathedrals, we shall feel it incumbent upon us to penetrate more deeply into the meaning of these few words. Truth does not mean mere lifeless accuracy of comprehension, but the right and appropriate regulation of life, a vital spiritual essence; it means the intrinsic value of existence in all its force and fulness. And beauty is the triumphant splendour which breaks forth when the hidden truth is revealed, when the external phenomenon is at all points the perfect expression of the inner essence. Perfection of expression, then, not merely superficial and external, but interior and contemporaneous with every step in the creation—can the essence of beauty be more profoundly and at the same time more briefly defined ?

Beauty cannot be appreciated unless this fact is borne in mind, and it is apprehended as the splendour of perfectly expressed intrinsic truth.

But there is a grave risk, which many people do not escape, of this order being reversed, and of beauty being placed before truth, or treated as entirely separate from the latter, the perfection of form from the content, and the expression from its substance and meaning. Such is the danger incurred by the æsthetic conception of the world, which ultimately degenerates into nerveless æstheticism.

No investigation of the æsthetic mind and ideas can be undertaken here. But we may premise that its primary characteristic is a more or less swift withdrawal from discussion of the reason for a thing's existence to the manner of it, from the content to the method of presentation, from the intrinsic value of the object to its value as a form, from the austerity of truth and the inflexible demands of morality to the relaxing harmony of beauty. This will happen more or less consistently, and more or less consciously, until everything terminates finally in a frame of mind which no longer recognises intrinsic truth, with its severe ' thus and not otherwise,' nor the moral idea with its unconditional ' either—or,' but which seeks for significance in form and expression alone. That which is objective, whether it is a natural object, a historical event, a man, a sorrow, a preference, a work, a legal transaction, knowledge, an idea, is merely viewed as a fact without significance. It serves as a pretext for expression, that is all.[1] Thus originates the

[1] Oscar Wilde's *Intentions* are quite clear on this point.

shadowy image of absolute form, a manner without a matter, a radiance without heat, a fact without force.[1]

People who think like this have lost the ability to grasp the profundity of a work of art, and the standard by which to measure its greatness. They no longer comprehend it as being what it is, as a victory and as an avowal. They do not even do justice to the form which is the exclusive object of their preoccupation ; for form means the expression of a substance, or the mode of life of an existent being.

Truth is the soul of beauty. People who do not understand what the one and the other are really worth turn their joyful play into mere empty trifling. There is something heroic in every great and genuine creation, in which the interior essence has won through opposition to its true expression. A good fight has been fought, in which some essential substance, conscious of the best elements within itself, has set aside that which is extraneous to itself, submitted all disorder and confusion to a strict discipline, and obeyed the laws of its own nature. A tremendous ebullition takes place, and an inner substance gives external testimony to its essence and to the essential message which it holds. But the æsthete looks upon all this as pointless trifling.

Nay, more. Æstheticism is profoundly shameless. All true beauty is modest. This word is not used in a superficial sense. It has no relation as to the suitability of this

---

[1] The writer has been reproached with treating the subject too simply in this exposition. He has deliberately shortened it for the sake of the fundamental idea, and has neglected many of its ramifications which should actually have been discussed. Yet after careful testing he finds no reason for altering his method of procedure. In a profounder sense, that which he here says is nevertheless justified.

or that for utterance, portrayal, or existence. What it means is that all expression has been impelled by an interior urge, justified by immutable standards, and permitted, even offered existence by the latter. This permission and obligation, however, only reside in the intrinsic truth of an entity or a genuine spiritual experience. Expression on the other hand for the sake of expression, self-elected as both matter and form, has no longer any value.

We are led yet further afield by these considerations. In spite of the most genuine impulse, and even when truth not only emphatically justifies the proceeding, but also imperatively demands it, all true inwardness still shrinks from self-revelation, just because it is full of all goodness. The desire for revelation, however, and the realisation that it is only in articulation that it can obtain release from the tyranny of silence, compel the expression of an inwardness ; yet it still shrinks from disclosure, because it fears that by this it will lose its noblest elements. The fulfilment of all inwardness lies in the instant when it discloses itself in a form appropriate to its nature. But it is immediately conscious of a painful reaction, of a sensation as of having irrevocably lost something inexpressibly precious.

This applies—or is it too sweeping a statement ?—to all genuine creative art. It is like a blush after the word, readily enough spoken, but followed by a secret reproach, an often incomprehensible pain, arising from depths till now unexplored ; it is like the quick compression of the lips which would give much to recall the hasty avowal. People who understand this are aware that further depths and modestly concealed riches still lie beyond that which, surrendering itself, has taken shape. This generosity, while at the same time the store remains undiminished, this advance, followed by withdrawal into resplendent fastnesses, this grappling with expression, triumphant expansion, and timid, dolorous contraction, together constitute the tenderest charm of beauty.

But all this—the restrained yet youthful fulness of candour—vanishes before the glance, at once disrespectful and obtuse, of those who seek after articulation for the sake of articulation, and after beauty for the sake of beauty.

Those who aspire to a life of beauty must, in the first place, strive to be truthful and good. If a life is true it will automatically become beautiful, just as light shines forth when flame is kindled. But if they seek after beauty in the first place, it will fare with them as it fared with Hedda Gabler, and in the end everything will become nauseating and loathsome.

In the same way—however strange it may sound—the creative artist must not seek after beauty in the abstract, not, that is, if he understands that beauty is something more than a certain grace of external form and a pleasing and elegant effect. He must, on the contrary, with all his strength endeavour to become true and just in himself, to apprehend truth and to live in and by it, and in this way fully realise both the internal and external world. And then the artist, as the enemy of all vanity and showiness, must express truth as it should be expressed, without the alteration of a single stroke or trait. It follows that his work, if he is an artist at all, will, and not only will, but *must* be beautiful. If, however, he tries to avoid the toilsome path of truth, and to distil form from form, that which he represents is merely empty illusion.

People who have not enjoyed—repulsive word, which

puts beauty on a par with a titbit, and originates from the worthless conception which we have just now censured— human perfection or the beauty of a work of art, but desire closer familiarity with it, must take the inner essence for their starting-point. They will be well advised to ignore expression and harmony of form at first, but to endeavour to penetrate instead to the inner truth of the vital essence. Viewed from this standpoint, the whole process by which the matter transposes itself into its form becomes apparent, and the spectators witness a miraculous flowering. This means that they are familiar with beauty, although perhaps they may not consciously recognise it for what it is, but are merely aware of a sentiment of perfect satisfaction at the visible and adequate fulfilment of an object or of an existence.

Beauty eludes those who pursue it for its own sake, and their life and work are ruined because they have sinned against the fundamental order of values. If a man, however, desires to live for truth alone, to be truthful in himself and to speak the truth, and if he keeps his soul open, beauty—in the shape of richness, purity, and vitality of form—will come to meet him, unsought and unexpected.

What profound penetration and insight was shown by Plato, the master of æsthetics, in his warnings against the dangers of excessive worship of beauty ! We need a new artist-seer to convince the young people of our day, who bend the knee in idolatrous homage before art and beauty, what must be the fruit of such perversion of the highest spiritual laws.

We must now refer what has already been propounded to the liturgy. There is a danger that in the liturgical sphere as well æstheticism may spread ; that the liturgy will first be the subject of general eulogy, then gradually its various treasures will be estimated at their æsthetic value, until finally the sacred beauty of the House of God comes to provide a delicate morsel for the connoisseur. Until, that is, the ' house of prayer ' becomes once more, in a different way, a ' den of thieves.' But for the sake of Him who dwells there and for that of our own souls, this must not be tolerated.

The Church has not built up the *Opus Dei* for the pleasure of forming beautiful symbols, choice language, and graceful, stately gestures, but she has done it—in so far as it is not completely devoted to the worship of God —for the sake of our desperate spiritual need. It is to give expression to the events of the Christian's inner life : the assimilation, through the Holy Ghost, of the life of the creature to the life of God in Christ ; the actual and genuine rebirth of the creature into a new existence ; the development and nourishment of this life, its stretching forth from God in the Blessed Sacrament and the means of grace, towards God in prayer and sacrifice ; and all this in the continual mystic renewal of Christ's life in the course of the ecclesiastical year. The fulfilment of all these processes by the set forms of language, gesture, and instruments, their revelation, teaching, accomplishment and acceptance by the faithful, together constitute the liturgy. We see, then, that it is primarily concerned with reality, with the approach of a real creature to a real God, and with the profoundly real and serious matter of redemption. There is here no question of creating beauty, but of finding salvation for sin-stricken humanity. Here truth is at stake, and the fate of the soul, and real—yes, ultimately the only real—life. All this it is which must be revealed, expressed, sought after, found, and imparted by every possible means and method; and when this is accomplished, lo ! it is turned into beauty.[1]

This is not a matter for amazement, since the principle here at work is the principle of truth and of mastery over form. The interior element has been expressed clearly and truthfully, the whole superabundance of life has found its utterance, and the fathomless profundities have been plainly mapped out. It is only to be expected that a gleam of the utmost splendour should shine forth at such a manifestation of truth.

For us, however, the liturgy must chiefly be regarded from the standpoint of salvation. We should steadfastly endeavour to convince ourselves of its truth and its importance in our lives. When we recite the prayers and psalms of the liturgy, we are to praise God, nothing more. When we assist at Holy Mass, we must know that we are close to the fount of all grace. When we are present at an ordination, the significance of the proceedings must lie for us in the fact that the grace of God has taken possession of a fragment of human life. We are not concerned here with the question of powerfully symbolic gestures, as if we were in a spiritual theatre, but we have to see that our real souls should approach a little nearer to the real God, for the sake of all our most personal, profoundly serious affairs.

For it is only thus that perception of liturgical beauty

[1] The Abbot of Marialaach rightly remarks in this connection, ' I stress the point that the liturgy has *developed* into a work of art ; it was not deliberately formed as such by the Church. The liturgy bore within itself so much of the seed of beauty that it was of itself bound to flower ultimately. But the internal principle which controlled the form of that flowering was the essence of Christianity.' (Herwegen, *Das Kunstprinzip der Liturgie*, p. 18, Paderborn, 1916.)

will be vouchsafed to us. It is only when we participate in liturgical action with the earnestness begotten of deep personal interest that we become aware why, and in what perfection, this vital essence is revealed. It is only when we premise the truth of the liturgy that our eyes are opened to its beauty.

The degree of perception varies, according to our æsthetic sensitiveness. Perhaps it will merely be a pleasant feeling of which we are not even particularly conscious, of the profound appropriateness of both language and actions for the expression of spiritual realities, a sensation of quiet spontaneity, a consciousness that everything is right and exactly as it should be. Then perhaps an offertory suddenly flashes in upon us, so that it gleams before us like a jewel. Or bit by bit the whole sweep of the Mass is revealed, just as from out the vanishing mist the peaks and summits and slopes of a mountain chain stand out in relief, shining and clear, so that we imagine we are looking at them for the first time. Or it may be that in the midst of prayer the soul will be pervaded by that gentle, blithe gladness which rises into sheer rapture. Or else the book will sink from our hands, while, penetrated with awe, we taste the meaning of utter and blissful tranquillity, conscious that the final and eternal verities which satisfy all longing have here found their perfect expression.

But these moments are fleeting, and we must be content to accept them as they come or are sent.

On the whole, however, and as far as everyday life is concerned, this precept holds good, ' Seek first the kingdom of God and His justice, and all else shall be added to you '—all else, even the glorious experience of beauty.

7

THE PRIMACY OF THE LOGOS OVER THE ETHOS

The liturgy exhibits one peculiarity which strikes as very odd those natures in particular which are generously endowed with moral energy and earnestness—and that is its singular attitude towards the moral order.

People of the type instanced above chiefly regret one thing in the liturgy, that its moral system has few direct relations with everyday life. It does not offer any easily transposable motives, or ideas realisable at first hand, for the benefit of our daily conflicts and struggles. A certain isolation, a certain remoteness from actual life characterise it; it is celebrated in the somewhat sequestered sphere of spiritual things. A contrast exists between the study, the factory, and the laboratory of to-day, between the arena of public and social life and the Holy Places of solemn, divine worship, between the intensely practical tendency of our time, which is opposed to life by its wholly material force and acrid harshness, and the lofty, measured domain of liturgical conceptions and determination, with its clearness and elevation of form.

From this it follows that we cannot directly translate into action that which the liturgy offers us. There will always be a constant need, then, for methods of devotion which have their origin in a close connection with modern life, and for the popular devotions by which the Church meets the special demands and requirements of actual existence, and which, since they directly affect the soul, are immediately productive of practical results.[1] The liturgy, on the contrary, is primarily occupied in forming the fundamental Christian temper. By it man is to be induced to determine correctly his essential relation to God, and to put himself right in regard to reverence for God, love and faith, atonement and the desire for sacrifice. As a result of this spiritual disposition, it follows that when action is required of him he will do what is right.

The question, however, goes yet deeper. What is the position of the liturgy generally to the moral order ? What is the quality of the relation in it of the will to knowledge, as of the value of truth to the value of goodness ? Or, to put it in two words, what is the relation in it of the Logos to the Ethos ? It will be necessary to go back somewhat in order to find the answer.

It is safe to affirm that the Middle Ages, in philosophy at least, answered the question as to the relation between these two fundamental principles by decisively ranking knowledge before will and the activity attendant upon the functioning of the latter. They gave the Logos precedence over the Ethos. That is proved by the way

[1] Both in this connection and in countless others we find demonstrated the absolute necessity of the extra-liturgical forms of spiritual exercise, the Rosary, the Stations of the Cross, popular devotions, meditation, etc. There could be no greater mistake than the attempt to build up liturgical life on an exclusively liturgical model. And it is equally mistaken merely to tolerate the other forms, because the ' lower classes ' need them, while setting the liturgy as the only possible pattern and guide before struggling humanity. Both are necessary. The one complements the other. Pride of place, however, belongs of course to the liturgy, because it is the official prayer of the Church.

(Cf. my book, *Der Kreuzweg unseres Hernn und Heilandes*, Introduction, Mainz, 1921.)

in which certain frequently discussed questions are answered,[1] and by the absolute priority which was assigned to the contemplative life over the active [2] ; this stands out as the fundamental attitude of the Middle Ages, which took the Hereafter as the constant and exclusive goal of all earthly striving.

Modern times brought about a great change. The great objective institutions of the Middle Ages—class solidarity, the municipalities, the Empire—broke up. The power of the Church was no longer, as formerly, absolute and temporal. In every direction individualism became more strongly pronounced and independent. This development was chiefly responsible for the growth of scientific criticism, and in a special manner the criticism of knowledge itself. The inquiry into the essence of know-ledge, which formally followed a constructive method, now assumes, as a result of the profound spiritual changes which have taken place, its characteristic critical form. Knowledge itself becomes questionable, and as a result the centre of gravity and the fulcrum of the spiritual life gradually shifts from knowledge to the will. The actions of the independent individual become increasingly important. In this way active life forces its way before the contemplative, the will before knowledge.

Even in science, which after all is essentially dependent

[1] Cf. the discussions on the significance of theology as to whether it is a ' pure ' science or one with an aim, that of bettering humanity ; upon the essence of eternal happiness, whether it ultimately consists in the con-templation of God or in the love of Him ; on the dependence of the will upon knowledge, and so on.

[2] It is significant that it was not until the seventeenth century, and then in the face of universal opposition, that active Orders for women were founded. The history of the Order of the Visitation is especially instruc-tive in this connection.

upon knowledge, a peculiar significance is assigned to the will. In place of the former penetration of guaranteed truth, of tranquil assimilation and discussion, there now develops a restless investigation of obscure, questionable truth. Instead of explanation and assimilation, education tends increasingly towards independent investigation. The entire scientific sphere exhibits an enterprising and aggressive tendency. It develops into a powerful, restlessly productive, labouring community.

This importance of the will has been scientifically formulated in the most conclusive manner by Kant. He recognised, side by side with the order of perception, of the world of things, in which the understanding alone is competent, the order of practicality, of freedom, in which the will functions. Arising out of the postulations of the will he admits the growth of a third order, the order of faith, as opposed to knowledge, the world of God and the soul. While the understanding is of itself incapable of asserting anything on these latter matters, because it is unable to verify them by the senses, it receives belief in their reality, and thus the final shaping of its conception of the world, from the postulations of the will which cannot exist and function without these highest data from which to proceed. This established the ' primacy of the will.' The will, together with the scale of moral values peculiar to it, has taken precedence of knowledge with its corresponding scale of values ; the Ethos has obtained the primacy over the Logos.

The ice having been broken, there now follows the entire course of philosophic development which sets, in the place of the pure will logically conceived by Kant, the psychological will, constituting the latter the unique rule of life—a development due to Fichte, Schopenhauer, and von Hartmann—until it finds its clearest expression in Nietzsche. He proclaims the ' will to power.' For him, truth is that which makes life sound and noble, leading humanity further towards the goal of the ' Superman.'

Such is the origin of pragmatism, by which truth is no longer viewed as an independent value in the case of a conception of the universe or in spiritual matters, but as the expression of the fact that a principle or a system benefits life and actual affairs, and elevates the character and stability of the will.[1] Truth is fundamentally, if not entirely—though here we overstep the field marked out for our consideration—a moral, though hardly a vital fact.

This predominance of the will and of the idea of its value gives the present day its peculiar character. It is the reason for its restless pressing forward, the stringent limiting of its hours of labour, the precipitancy of its enjoyment ; hence, too, the worship of success, of strength, of action ; hence the striving after power, and generally the exaggerated opinion of the value of time, and the compulsion to exhaust oneself by activity till the end. This is the reason, too, why spiritual organisations such as the old contemplative orders, which formerly were automatically accepted by spiritual life everywhere and which were the darlings of the orthodox world, are not infrequently misunderstood even by Catholics, and have to be defended by their friends against the reproach of

---

[1] This tendency has also influenced Catholic thought. A great deal of modernistic thought endeavours to make theological truth—dogma—dependent upon Christian life and to estimate its importance not as a standard of truth, but as a value in life.

idle trifling. And if it is true that this attitude of mind has already become firmly established in Europe, whose culture is rooted in the distant past, it is doubly true where the New World is concerned. There it comes to light unconcealed and unalloyed. The practical will is everywhere the decisive factor, and the Ethos has complete precedence over the Logos, the active side of life over the contemplative.

What is the position of Catholicism in relation to this development ? It must be premised that the best elements of every period and of every type of mind can and will find their fulfilment in this Religion, which is truly capable of being all things to all men. So it has been possible to adapt the tremendous development of power during the last five centuries in Catholic life, and to summon ever fresh aspects from its inexhaustible store. A long investigation would be needed if we were to point out how many highly valuable personalities, tendencies, activities and views have been called forth from Catholic life as a result of this responsiveness to the needs of all ages. But it must be pointed out that an extensive, biased, and lasting predominance of the will over knowledge is profoundly at variance with the Catholic spirit.

Protestantism presents, in its various forms, ranging from the strong tendency to the extreme of free speculation, the more or less Christian version of this spirit, and Kant has rightly been called its philosopher. It is a spirit which has step by step abandoned objective religious truth, and has increasingly tended to make conviction a matter of personal judgment, feeling, and experience. In this way truth has fallen from the objective plane to the level of a relative and fluctuating value. As a result, the will has been obliged to assume the leadership. When the believer no longer possesses any fundamental principles, but only an experience of faith as it affects him personally, the one solid and recognisable fact is no longer a body of dogma which can be handed on in tradition, but the right action as a proof of the right spirit. In this connection there can be no talk of spiritual metaphysics in the real sense of the word. And when knowledge has nothing ultimately to seek in the Above, the roots of the will and of feeling are in their turn loosened from their adherence to knowledge. The relation with the supertemporal and eternal order is thereby broken. The believer no longer stands in eternity, but in time, and eternity is merely connected with time through the medium of conviction, but not in a direct manner. Religion becomes increasingly turned towards the world, and cheerfully secular. It develops more and more into a consecration of temporal human existence in its various aspects, into a sanctification of earthly activity, of vocational labour, of communal and family life, and so on.

Everyone, however, who has debated these matters at any considerable length clearly perceives the unwholesomeness of such a conception of spiritual life, and the flagrance of its contradiction of all fundamental spiritual principles. It is untrue, and therefore contrary to Nature in the deepest sense of the word. Here is the real source of the terrible misery of our day. It has perverted the sacred order of Nature. It was Goethe who really shook the latter when he made the doubting Faust write, not ' In the beginning was the Word,' but ' In the beginning was the Deed.'

While life's centre of gravity was shifting from the

Logos to the Ethos, life itself was growing increasingly unrestrained. Man's will was required to be responsible for him. Only one Will can do this, and that is creative in the absolute sense of the word, *i.e.*, it is the Divine Will.[1] Man, then, was endowed with a quality which presumes that he is God. And since he is not, he develops a spiritual cramp, a kind of weak fit of violence, which takes effect often in a tragic, and sometimes (in the case of lesser minds) even a ludicrous manner. This presumption is guilty of having put modern man into the position of a blind person groping his way in the dark, because the fundamental force upon which it has based life—the will— is blind. The will can function and produce, but cannot see. From this is derived the restlessness which nowhere finds tranquillity. Nothing is left, nothing stands firm, everything alters, life is in continual flux ; it is a constant struggle, search, and wandering.

Catholicism opposes this attitude with all its strength. The Church forgives everything more readily than an attack on truth. She knows that if a man falls, but leaves truth unimpaired, he will find his way back again. But if he attacks the vital principle, then the sacred order of life is demolished. Moreover, the Church has constantly viewed with the deepest distrust every ethical conception of truth and of dogma. Any attempt to base the truth of a dogma merely on its practical value is essentially un-

---

[1] Yet even here reason affirms that God is not merely an Absolute Will, but, at the same time, truth and goodness. Revelation seals this, as it does every form of spiritual perception, by showing us that in the Blessed Trinity the ' first thing ' is the begetting of the Son through the recognition of the Father, and the ' second ' (according to thought, of course, not according to time) is the breathing forth of the Holy Ghost through the love of Both.

Catholic.[1] The Church represents truth—dogma—as an absolute fact, based upon itself, independent of all confirmation from the moral or even from the practical sphere. Truth is truth because it is truth. The attitude of the will to it, and its action towards it, is of itself a matter of indifference to truth. The will is not required to prove truth, nor is the latter obliged to give an account of itself to the will, but the will has to acknowledge itself as perfectly incompetent before truth. It does not create the latter, but it finds it. The will has to admit that it is blind and needs the light, the leadership, and the organising formative power of truth. It must admit as a fundamental principle the primacy of knowledge over the will, of the Logos over the Ethos.[2]

This ' primacy ' has been misunderstood. It is not a question of a priority of value or of merit. Nor is there any suggestion that knowledge is more important than action in human life. Still less does a desire exist to direct people as to the advisability of setting about their affairs with prayer or with action. The one is just as valuable and meritorious as the other. It is partly a question of disposition ; the tone of a man's life will accentuate either knowledge or action ; and the one type of disposition is worth as much as the other. The ' Primacy ' is far rather a matter of culture—philosophy, and indeed it consists of

[1] Here nothing is said, of course, against the endeavour to exhibit the value of dogma in the abstract, and that of the single dogmatic truth for life. On the contrary, this can never be done forcibly enough.

[2] This is said of knowledge, not of comprehension ; of the primacy of knowledge over the practical, of the contemplative over the active life, in the way understood by the Middle Ages, even if it lacks the latter's cultural-historical characteristics. On the other hand, it is impossible for us to free ourselves sufficiently from the domination of pure comprehension, as it has endured for half a century.

the question as to which value in the whole of culture and of human life the leadership will be assigned, and which therefore will determine the decisive tendency; it is a precedence of order, therefore, of leadership, not of merit, significance, or even of frequency.

But if we concern ourselves further with the question, the idea occurs that the conception of the Primacy of the Logos over the Ethos could not be the final one. Perhaps it should be put thus: in life as a whole, precedence does not belong to action, but to existence. What ultimately matters is not activity, but development. The roots of and the perfection of everything lie, not in time, but in eternity. Finally, not the moral, but the metaphysical conception of the world is binding, not the worth-judgment, but the import-judgment, not struggle, but worship.

These trains of thought, however, trespass beyond the limits of this little book. The further question—if a final precedence must not be allotted to love—seems to be linked with a different chain of thought. Its solution perhaps lies within the possibilities we have already discussed. When one knows, for instance, that for a time truth is the decisive standard, it is still not quite established whether truth insists upon love or upon frigid majesty; the Ethos can be an obligation of the law, as with Kant, or the obligation of creative love. And even face to face with existence it is still an open question whether this obligation is a final rigid inevitability, or if it is love transcending all measure, in which the impossible itself becomes possible, to which hope can appeal against all hope. That is what is meant by the question whether love is not the greatest of these. Indeed, it is.

Nothing less than this was announced by the 'good tidings.'

In this sense, too, as far as the primacy of truth—but 'truth in love'—is concerned, the present question is to be resolved.

As soon as this is done the foundation of spiritual health is established. For the soul needs absolutely firm ground on which to stand. It needs a support by which it can raise itself, a sure external point beyond itself, and that can only be supplied by truth. The knowledge of pure truth is the fundamental factor of spiritual emancipation. 'The truth shall make you free.' [1] The soul needs that spiritual relaxation in which the convulsions of the will are stilled, the restlessness of struggle quietened, and the shrieking of desire silenced; and that is fundamentally and primarily the act of intention by which thought perceives truth, and the spirit is silent before its splendid majesty.

In dogma, the fact of absolute truth, inflexible and eternal, entirely independent of a basis of practicality, we possess something which is inexpressibly great. When the soul becomes aware of it, it is overcome by a sensation as of having touched the mystic guarantee of universal sanity; it perceives dogma as the guardian of all existence, actually and really the rock upon which the universe rests. 'In the beginning was the Word '—the Logos. . . .

For this reason the basis of all genuine and healthy life is a contemplative one. No matter how great the energy of the volition and action and striving may be, it must rest on the tranquil contemplation of eternal, unchangeable truth. This attitude is rooted in eternity. It is peaceful, it has that interior restraint which is a victory over life.

[1] John viii. 32.

It is not in a hurry, but has time. It can afford to wait and to develop.

This spiritual attitude is really Catholic. And if it is also a fact, as some maintain, that Catholicism is in many aspects, as compared with the other denominations, 'backward,' by all means let it be. Catholicism could not join in the furious pursuit of the unchained will, torn from its fixed and eternal order. But it has in exchange preserved something that is irreplaceably precious, for which, if it were to recognise it, the non-Catholic spiritual world would willingly exchange all that it has ; and this is the primacy of the Logos over the Ethos, and by this, harmony with the established and immutable laws of all existence.

Although as yet the liturgy has not been specifically mentioned, everything which has been said applies to it. In the liturgy the Logos has been assigned its fitting precedence over the will.[1] Hence the wonderful power of relaxation proper to the liturgy, and its deep reposefulness. Hence its apparent consummation entirely in the contemplation, adoration and glorification of Divine Truth. This is also the explanation of the fact that the liturgy is apparently so little disturbed by the petty troubles and needs of everyday life. It also accounts for the comparative rareness of its attempts at direct teaching and direct inculcation of virtue. The liturgy has something in itself reminiscent of the stars, of their eternally fixed and even course, of their inflexible order, of their profound silence, and of the infinite space in which they are poised. It is only in appearance, however, that the liturgy is so

[1] Because it reposes upon existence, upon the essential, and even upon existence in love, as I hope to be able to demonstrate upon a future occasion.

detached and untroubled by the actions and strivings and moral position of men. For in reality it knows that those who live by it will be true and spiritually sound, and at peace to the depths of their being; and that when they leave its sacred confines to enter life they will be men of courage.